FORTIFY

a step toward recovery

FORTIFY
a step toward recovery

WRITTEN BY

FIGHT THE NEW DRUG

in conjunction with a team of professionals in
psychology, neuroscience,
addiction recovery, and content delivery

O.W.L.
PUBLISHING

www.fortifyprogram.org
www.fightthenewdrug.org

a step toward recovery

The problem of pornography addiction has never been worse. With easy access to the most extreme pornographic material at the tip of our fingers we are facing something our parents never did. In the palm of our hand we can be exposed to images, messages, and ideas that cripple our potential and distort our very nature.

Fortify was specifically designed to help young people facing an addiction to pornography eventually reach long-lasting freedom. In this book you will find the tools, education, and resources necessary to help you or someone you love overcome this addiction.

**Sign up for our free online program at
www.fortifyprogram.org**

To all the brave, courageous, smart, and passionate Fighters out there making a difference.

FOR·TI·FY / fôrtəfī/(v)

1. To make strong, or stronger.
2. To strengthen a place, making it defensible and more secure, as by building walls, digging trenches, etc.
3. To strengthen or make an individual strong or stronger.
4. To impart physical strength or endurance to; invigorate or reinforce someone mentally or physically.
5. To support or confirm an argument with facts.

TABLE OF CONTENTS

CHAPTER 1: FORTIFY ORIENTATION

CHAPTER 2: RECOGNIZING THE ENEMY

CHAPTER 3: BASIC TRAINING

CHAPTER 4: FORTIFY YOURSELF

CHAPTER 5: FORTIFY YOUR RELATIONSHIPS

CHAPTER 6: FORTIFY YOUR WORLD

CHAPTER 7: RISE AND RISE AGAIN

CHAPTER 8: BECOMING A FIGHTER

FOREWORD

The Fortify Program is a self-directed recovery program created and developed by Fight the New Drug, a grassroots, youth oriented, non-profit organization dedicated to raising awareness on the harmful effects of pornography.

As we have traveled across the country raising awareness on the harms of pornography, we have been overwhelmed with the sheer volume of teens who have reached out to us, confessing that they needed help in overcoming their struggle with pornography addiction. They spoke of how they had nowhere to turn for help and that they felt alone in their fight. Over time we became determined to provide tools and resources for the thousands of young people who have asked us for help as well as those that are silently struggling.

We teamed up with psychologists, neurologists, therapists, and other mental health experts to create a program that educates and empowers individuals to break free of pornography addiction.

The Fortify Program dives deep into the scientific reasons for addiction and the porn industry's tactics to create life-long customers. It has been designed to eventually help users reach long-lasting freedom by providing the tools, education, and resources necessary to overcome this addictive behavior.

It is important to know and understand that there are levels and degrees of pornography addiction. Some of you are dealing with an addiction that makes it difficult to have a relationship, be social, or even leave the house. There are others who feel like it is just a bad habit or something they want to stop before they lose control. Some are using porn a few times a year, others a few times a month, and some feel compelled to use several times a day. Everyone who is looking for help from this book has a different story and different needs with regard to their porn use.

Even with these vast differences and degrees of use, this book uses the blanket term of addiction to describe compulsive pornography use. Wherever you may land on that spectrum, the Fortify Program will help you as you begin your process of recovery. No one but you can determine how deep your trench is, and a commitment to completing this program will assist you as you begin your process of recovery and work toward lasting change.

WELCOME
TO THE
FIGHT!

Read and apply this book, but don't stop there!
Join us in the fight against pornography!

#FIGHTTHENEWDRUG

CHAPTER ONE >>>

FORTIFY
ORIENTATION

DISCLAIMER:

For use in this program the term **pornography addiction** is used more broadly to cover any unwanted behaviors resulting from pornography use. That could mean something different for everyone. For example, some might be dealing with a bad habit while others are dealing with an extreme process of addiction. Regardless of where one might be, the Fortify Program was created to allow individuals to take a step closer toward long-lasting recovery.

A STEP IN THE RIGHT DIRECTION

Welcome to *Fortify*. We're glad you found us. Although we can't know your exact experience, feelings, and thoughts, we've spent a lot of time with others who have faced some of the same challenges that led you here.

If you're anything like them, you've probably worried about what went wrong in the past: "I can't believe I'm here. How did I get to this place? I'm not sure anything is going to change."

You may also have fears about your future: "Maybe I've been doing this too long. Maybe I've blown it. What if I can't beat this thing?"

And then you have this moment—a new start, a fresh beginning. No matter what happened yesterday, last month, or last year, guess what: right now, you're reading this book.

That says something about you. And if we have anything to say about it, it will also mean something about your future.

But for now, let's not fast-forward too much into tomorrow. Let's stick with today. And for today, just the fact that you're here—that you're reading this book—is worth celebrating a little bit. Think about it: with everything else that you could be doing right now, you chose to take time and check out this program.

That's no small thing. In fact, it's a big deal, and we're really glad you're here. We've got lots to talk about up ahead, but let's focus on one point for now: no matter how much or how long you've struggled, no matter how desperate or stuck you may feel right now, this is a new day. We're not being cheesy here, it's really true; no other moment that came before is exactly like this one.

You've just done something most people in your situation aren't brave enough to do: you've recognized that there is a problem, and you're doing something about it. Well done—seriously!

But you didn't come here just to get a pat on the back or a pep talk. You showed up because your life has been entangled and hijacked by something you can't control very well—or at all. You're here because you're tired of feeling that way and you're ready for something different, something more true to who you really are and what you want out of life.

That's why we're here too—because we also believe you deserve better. And we're going to give absolutely everything we've got to help you find that. So let's do this! Wherever you are, no matter where that is, it's the *perfect* place to begin.

⊛ ACTION

Before diving into the rest of this book, will you do us a favor? Do something to celebrate your decision to start *Fortify*. We're serious. If we were there with you, we'd grab a bucket of Ben and Jerry's ice cream and pick up your favorite movie. Do something, anything, to recognize this moment as a new one.

WHO YOU ARE VS. WHERE YOU ARE

While everyone's situation is different, most people facing an addiction like this one have gone back to using over and over—sometimes for many years. After a while, it's normal to start wondering whether this isn't just who you are. The same thoughts come up for most addictions: "Maybe I'm just a drunk," or "Doesn't this drug help me be who I really am?" You've probably heard similar ideas about porn: "Oh yeah, it's just a teenager thing"; "All guys are into that"; or "This is who I am."

So is that true? Some people sure want it to be—they hope it's true and really try to believe it. How about this: what if we just stuck with the facts—with our experience as it actually happens and with things as they really are?

After using porn again one night, a friend of ours told us that he turned off his computer to try and sleep. Sensing again the numbness and heaviness that always comes after using, he stopped and sat down on the floor: "This is not who I really am!" he cried in the dark. "And this is not the person I want to be. *This is not me!*"

It's much easier, of course, to say the opposite—to look around at our life and our media habits and just say, "This is my identity. It's who I am."

We're here to tell you something different. We're here to tell you straight up that there is a big difference between where you are and who you are.

It's true—you are here. You've been doing this stuff, maybe for a long time. That is *where you are.* But that doesn't mean that is *who you are.* In fact, this whole addiction may completely contradict who you really are!

Have you ever had a moment like the one we just talked about? A moment when you sensed—even just barely— that you are *better* than this? That this stuff is not really you—and may even go against who you actually are.

If you haven't had that moment, keep searching; you can. We promise.

For those of you who *have* already felt this—you probably also know how easy it is to fall into another trap. As if facing addiction isn't hard enough, we often add to the burden by telling ourselves some story about how we're completely broken, stupid, or worthless. Maybe you currently believe something like this. Maybe you even believe that reading this book is a sign you're a weak person deep down. We disagree—big time!

Whatever personal worries you may be carrying around, however mixed up you may feel, this is one point we want to make very clear: *you* are not the *primary* cause of this addiction.

All our obsessing about internal problems misses one pretty big part of the picture. It's called *The World*. And you are living in it. You're dwelling in a society that aggressively sets people up for the struggle you're facing. And if that is true, then maybe we should stop hammering ourselves so hard for being weak and pathetic. Maybe we should look at actual scientific explanations for why addiction happens in the first place.

To sum it up, no matter how long you have struggled or how stuck you may feel, *you are not your addiction*. Someone once said, "As long as you are breathing, there is more right with you than there is wrong," (Kabat-Zinn, 2005). Are you hearing us? Once again, you are not your addiction. You are much more than that, and that's how we see you.

In the end, the purpose of this book isn't to change you into somebody else. Instead, our aim is to help you reclaim and become again who you are and always have been, even if you forgot that for a while.

⭐ ACTION

Go back through pictures you have of yourself from the past and find one that captures the person you really are, deep down—beneath these challenges. Try to find a photo that reflects your true personality and feelings—before the addiction impacted you—even if that means going back to baby pictures. Once you find a good photo, post it somewhere in your room where you can see it. If you want, try posting a picture of one of your heroes as well—someone you look up to, someone that represents the type of person you hope to become. That could be a family member, a fictional superhero, or a real-life legend. The point is that you will have a strong visual reminder of who you really are—deep down—and who you want to become.

SCIENTIFIC EXPLANATIONS OF ADDICTION

We talked in the last section about who you really are. Now let's talk a bit more about where you are. In an upcoming chapter, we'll be going through different patterns in the world around us that set people up for addiction. From sleep deficiency and high levels of stress, to health and family problems, it's no surprise that many end up looking for some way to numb out.

What is a bit surprising, though, is how hard it can be to walk away from addictive habits once you've gone there. What is it that draws us back to things like drugs, tobacco, or alcohol—or pornography—even when we know they're hurting us?

As we just finished saying, it's not because people are stupid or weak. There is an actual scientific explanation as to why addiction happens, and it starts with the brain.

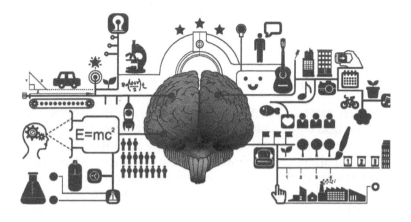

The brain is the powerhouse of the body. It's one of the most important things that makes you who you are. It allows you to choose what you will and won't do, and ultimately shapes who you become. So it's pretty important that we protect it. There are a lot of things that we can do to hurt or damage the brain, of course. We've all probably lost a few brain cells—whether from a bad fall, a helmet-to-helmet hit in football, wrecking hard on a mountain bike trail, or getting a roundhouse kick to the face by Chuck Norris. OK, maybe not that last one— you'd be dead. But we're not here to talk about *that* kind of harm to the brain.

In this program we're going to explore another kind of harm to the brain, the kind that comes from the inside, similar to the kind of damage caused by using things like hard drugs. So let's dig in and talk about this a little more.

Let's start by rewinding back to earlier in your life.

Think back on the time when you were younger—before you ever saw any pornography: Did you feel your day was ruined if you could not use pornography? Did you feel nervous, uncomfortable, or unable to concentrate because you could not check out a video?

Of course not. Your life went on perfectly normal as a non–porn viewer. You were able to get on with your life without giving the slightest thought to porn.

But then you tried it. And, like first-time smokers or drinkers, the body got a shock. Viewing pornography triggers a release of pleasure chemicals, such as dopamine, into what is called the "reward pathway" of the brain—the same pathway that fires up when you do something good that makes you happy, like hanging out with friends, eating your favorite meal, or riding a roller coaster. The difference here is that with harmful behaviors, chemicals get released in unnatural ways and at unhealthy levels.

REWARD PATHWAY

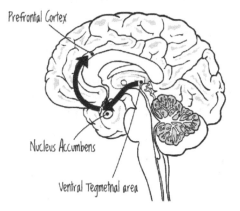

At first, your brain wasn't prepared for that chemical hit, so you probably felt sick, excited, or shocked during that first exposure. But over time, as you continued to use, the body got so used to those unhealthy chemical levels that it started to demand more and more of what you had started feeding it.

It's like Morgan Spurlock, the guy who ate McDonald's for 30 days in the documentary *Super Size Me*. At first he got really sick; but after a while his body got used to all the grease and fat he was eating, and even began craving and demanding it.

If a Big Mac can get demanding, it's not hard to imagine the same pattern with other things—including porn. And that's just what happens. Users go from not needing porn, to trying it, to wanting it, and eventually to needing it.

One of the main reasons addiction can be so hard to quit is that life never stops being challenging. Once we're accustomed to coping with difficult situations by escaping through an addiction, when something negative or uncomfortable arises, such as disappointment, stress, or loneliness, the brain can become trained like a puppy-dog to see the drug, alcohol, porn—whatever—as a solution.

As you keep going back to any harmful substance again and again, your brain builds up a tolerance and dependency on that overload of chemicals to the point where your brain demands more of it, more and more often, just to feel sort-of normal. That, my friend, is how addiction works. It hijacks your brain's natural appetites and slowly starts to take over your life, robbing you of your freedom to make your own choices.

Not cool.

SCIENCE CATCHING UP WITH TRUTH

So if porn is as addictive as other drugs, why aren't people talking about it? Unfortunately, history has shown that it can take years and even generations before a society understands the effects of addictive substances. As obvious as it sounds now that tobacco, alcohol, and drugs can cause serious harm, it took many years for people to believe they were dangerous—sometimes even after studies had shown how much damage they could cause.

For example, in the late 1800s, cocaine was considered an excellent cure for many health problems, including toothaches. Lloyd Manufacturing Co. called their product Cocaine Toothache Drops, which were available over the counter from 1885 to 1914. Have you ever had a toothache? Imagine hearing your doctor say, "Here's some cocaine; give it a try. It'll make you feel great. It'll make you forget you have teeth!" Sounds crazy, right?

So why do you think this product was taken off the shelves? Because now we know better—science finally caught up with truth.

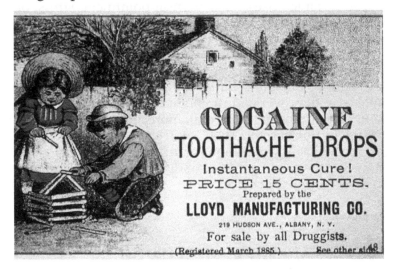

It happened again with alcohol. Many companies advertised that nursing mothers should drink alcohol so that the benefits of the alcohol would pass through their body to their nursing child. Makes no sense, right?

As you can imagine, after seeing a bunch of drunken babies stumbling around mid-crawl, they stopped doing that too.

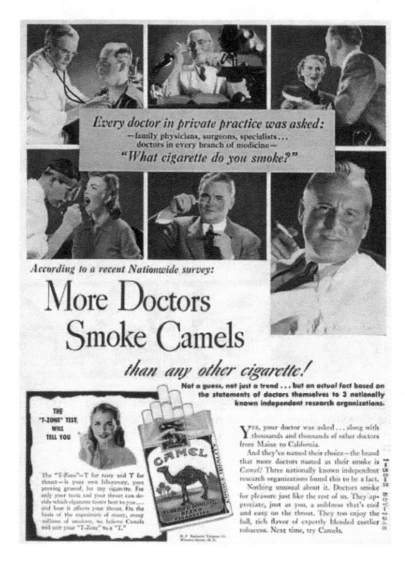

Another example of how we've gotten it wrong in the past is with tobacco. Not that long ago, doctors actually *prescribed* smoking because it "soothed the nerves and cleaned out the lungs." Well, it sure does something to the lungs, but it doesn't clean them out. Once again, we had to learn a lesson the hard way.

In each case—cocaine, alcohol, and tobacco—science had to catch up with truth. It was always true that those things were harmful, but it took a while for everyone to realize it.

Let's fast forward to our day. Guess what: we are learning a similar lesson with pornography. For many years, it was common to hear that pornography was a harmless pastime, and there was no reason to be worried. Not anymore. And this isn't just about opinion—not with what we have learned about the brain. Studies are showing that pornography can be just as addictive as other drugs and extremely harmful. Is this new to you? Have you ever compared pornography addiction to a drug addiction?

The reason this comparison makes sense is that scientists have learned that not all addictions come from chemicals you put into your body. Did you catch that? *Not all addictions come from chemicals you put into your body.*

From gambling, shopping, and thrill seeking, to video games, Internet use, and pornography, we now know that drugs aren't the only thing that can cause a chemical overload in the brain (Ghilan, 2012).

One of our Fighters on the East Coast who had dealt with several drug addictions as a teenager and later suffered from a serious addiction to pornography told us, "It wasn't until I paid attention to the symptoms of my pornography addiction that I realized that they were nearly identical to the symptoms I was having with drugs."

Understanding what addiction does to the brain may help us see how it is influencing our actions and overall life. To be specific, viewing pornography releases a flood of chemicals our bodies usually reserve for positive activities—such as dopamine, oxytocin, norepinephrine, and serotonin—into the reward pathway of the brain. The overexposure of these chemicals can influence things like self-control, aggression, ability to focus, and other physical appetites, along with general ability to feel pleasure and respond to pain.

This may cause you to have a harder time controlling your anger or dealing with stress. Your eating habits may change. Your ability to enjoy regular things, such as hanging out with friends, listening to music, spending time with family, or playing sports, may diminish because you feel depressed or numb. However fun they used to be, these activities may no longer feel satisfying after coming to expect the rush of dopamine and norepinephrine that accompanies pornography use. And what happens when you want to have a real romantic relationship? We'll talk much more about this later, but we'll summarize it in one word: problems.

Technology today has made it easier to drown our brain in those chemicals over and over again. That unnatural amount of chemicals, once again, is what causes the addiction. When it comes to the brain, then, addiction is addiction. It doesn't matter if it's cocaine or pornography—the effects on the brain are the same.

After seeing porn's negative effects in your own life, you've probably made an effort to quit and not use porn anymore. But after trying to resist for a while, you go back. You try to stop again. Then you go back again—over and over, again and again. You're stuck. In a literal sense, you are no longer completely free. Your actions and choices are now mandated, controlled, and driven. Even if you want to leave the addiction, you may still feel helpless against its power over you.

Do you know what the Latin root for the word "addiction" is? This is interesting; check it out. It means "dictator." A dictator is a ruler with total power over a country.

How would you like to live in a country controlled by a dictator, where your freedom was severely restricted? What would you feel in that situation?

We'll tell you our answer: We wouldn't put up with it. We'd get angry and rebel. When our freedom to choose what we most want is restricted by anyone (or anything), anger makes sense. So what do you say? Have you ever joined a rebellion? Are you with us? Maybe it's actually time to get a little ticked at being controlled and forced to keep doing something you really don't want to do deep down.

You make the call. If you're in, we're ready!

QUICK QUESTION:
Did you already know any of these scientific reasons behind why pornography can be as addictive as other drugs? Does that awareness change how you see your own experience with pornography?

GOOD NEWS ABOUT THE BRAIN

"Well hold on," you might be saying. "If my brain is involved in this problem, is change even possible?" After a long time—even years—of struggling, we don't blame you for asking. If you're feeling especially discouraged about change, this section is for you.

To help someone who is feeling down, we often say things like, "Stay hopeful"; "try to have a good attitude"; and "don't give up." We agree with this advice and like to hear it sometimes ourselves. Other times, though, it can be very hard to believe that anything is really going to change.

So today, we've got a concrete, rock-solid reason for you to stay hopeful. Are you ready? Here it is: your brain and body are remarkably changeable. Did you know that? Almost no one did until the 1990s when some new scientific discoveries took place. Brain researchers used to believe that the brain was pretty much fixed and unchangeable. People knew that the brains of younger children changed and developed, of course. But the belief at the time was that once you became an adult, your brain became set in place with fixed neurochemical levels and stable brain pathways. Basically, this meant if you messed your brain up when you were young the damage remained permanent for the rest of your life.

Scientists don't believe this about the brain anymore. The biggest discovery in neuroscience in the last two decades is a juicy word: *neuroplasticity*, "neuro" meaning brain and "plasticity" meaning changeability.

What this refers to is your brain's ability to change with each thing you do. Like a never-ending game of Tetris, the brain is constantly laying down new layers and pathways based on the choices we make.

Each time you learn something, try something different, or experience something new, a fresh connection is forged and formed in your brain—with constant rewiring happening every moment based on your actions.

This happens, of course, with pornography use as well. Over a long time, pornography use can start to literally rewire your brain, making it more and more difficult for you to resist using.

But the opposite is also true! As we begin to live differently, we forge new pathways in the brain. And as we leave old habits behind, the old pathways get grown over like a boring hiking trail no one uses anymore.

Pretty good news, right? Just in case you missed it, here it is again: No matter how deep you are into this addiction and no matter how long you've been struggling, there is hope. As long as you don't give up the fight your brain can change and rewire itself back to a healthy state over time.

FIGHTING SMART

So what is it going to take for you or anyone who struggles with pornography addiction to become truly free? You may not be surprised to hear this from us: you're going to have to fight. *We're* going to have to fight. Freedom in any form never comes easy, not without a price.

But it's not like you haven't tried to get out of this before, right? Have you ever tried to just rally yourself to stop by saying, "ENOUGH! No more!" in an effort to make some kind of dramatic, night-and-day shift? Most of us have. Like the Incredible Hulk, we sometimes think we can just clench our fists, gather all our willpower, and suddenly change ourselves by sheer force.

You know what we're talking about: I've got to just try harder! If I put my mind to it, I can do anything. Just work harder! Do more! Resist more! Have more willpower!

And we really think that's all it's going to take! Have you ever had a hard time getting to sleep? On those nights, have you ever tried harder to make yourself go to sleep? What happens? Most times, that only makes it worse, right? Like quicksand, sometimes the harder we struggle against something, the deeper we're pulled into it.

In a similar way, those who run directly at an addiction—trying to battle it back with sheer willpower and force their behavior to change—almost always become exhausted before long. For a day or two after a dramatic declaration of "No More!" we pat ourselves on the back for having iron willpower and being a completely new person. Then, when that new person isn't looking, we're often right back where we started.

We're not interested in prompting any more Incredible Hulk moments for you. We've got something better in mind. Don't get us wrong: effort is super important and full recovery won't happen without investing everything you've got. But what makes all the difference is how exactly this effort is spent.

If we're serious about getting you to a new place, it's going to require a certain kind of effort and a different way of fighting—one that goes deeper than behavior alone, one that takes the full picture of your life seriously, and one that takes your mind and heart as much as your muscles.

In the chapters ahead we'll be exploring all of this and much more. Everything we talk about will prepare you to fight this problem in a new and more powerful way—a way that leads, slowly but surely, to real freedom one day. Learning how to fight smart won't be easy and it will take some time and patience on your part, but that's OK. Trust us. It will be worth it.

> **QUICK QUESTION:**
> What have you tried in the past to help you overcome your addiction to pornography? How has it worked so far?

HOPEFUL AND REALISTIC EXPECTATIONS

While reading a book like *Fortify*, it's easy to think, "Hey, maybe I've found my answer. I'll just finish reading and be free of this!" Let's talk about that for a minute. Will sitting and reading a book suddenly flip a switch in your brain and free you?

You probably already know the answer: it won't. But

if you're wondering whether the specific strategies and plans we'll be exploring together can help you get out of this, then the answer is yes, they definitely can! Thousands of people have traveled this same path and quit this stuff for good. And you're next!

Like we talked about earlier, getting free from this trap will require something more than a burst of superhuman effort. Instead of just fighting harder, it will take fighting smarter—learning to maneuver and approach this problem in a new way, a way that gives you the upper hand.

If you're interested in moving in this direction, then buckle up. Any serious battle starts with some serious training. Up ahead, we'll start to equip and prepare you as a Fighter with everything you'll need. We'll give you some strategies that can help you in moments of possible weakness and practices to strengthen your home base. After this basic training, we'll dig deeper to get at the roots of addiction and help you fortify your life as a whole. We'll also talk about ways to keep going when things get tough, and discuss strategies to ultimately regain freedom in your life.

Your own pathway to freedom will depend on the good things you've already got in your life. This will be unique for each of us—and can include family relationships, hobbies, values, passions, faith, etc. As we explore the many contributors to addiction, we'll ultimately be helping you create your own personal plan to guide you out of it—a battle strategy for your own life. This long-term plan will be a crucial tool on the path to authentic, lasting freedom—the kind that won't wear off in a couple weeks like a cheap spray tan.

As you already know, progress in this war won't happen overnight. Real change is usually deep and gradual rather than dramatic; quiet rather than fancy; and based on long, sustained work rather than just an intense burst of energy. But again, our goal is not to get you excited for a couple of weeks to do better. That might give you a buzz for a while, but it wouldn't last.

We're here to talk about the roots of this problem—what underlies it and sustains its power over time—as well as what it takes to foster a deep and stable change. We didn't just write this book in our garage with a few friends. We collaborated with a team of professionals in many different fields of expertise.

What you will read draws on literally hundreds of research studies, all focused on getting at the roots of this addiction.

By taking a good, hard look into your life—the things you do or don't do on a daily basis—and by making some key adjustments, you will be able to fortify your life successfully and decrease your vulnerability to the problem itself. As this happens, you may be surprised to discover some real power and control over your own life returning once again. And what about when the urges hit? With a little help from some new skills we'll be practicing, you can also learn to eventually move past any temptations that come your way. Doesn't that sound good?

No matter how controlled you feel right now or how many battles you are losing, you determine who wins the larger war. In many cases, it's going to take a lot of time, practice, and help from others, but it all starts with your choice to move forward. It won't be easy, but as long as you don't give up, good things will happen—we promise.

There are many differences between each of you. Some may have been addicted for a brief period of time and others for much longer. Some are older, others younger. Some are guys, others are girls. We've been aware of these differences while developing this program, and we've made sure the ideas we will discuss are applicable to anyone.

Reaching lasting recovery is our hope for you. Since everyone's situation is different, we're not even going to put a
timeline to it. But faster or slower, sooner or later, we can
assure you this: things can get better; you can become stronger; and freedom—in the fullest sense—is within reach.

You probably won't win every battle that lies ahead; but
keep in mind, if you move this direction the war is yours
to win. And when it gets difficult, remember that you've
got thousands of other Fighters by your side, heading in
the same direction. We're in this together. And we hope
you will feel the strength of being part of a growing army
fighting the same battle. And make no mistake: we're in
this to win, and we won't be stopped.

BATTLE STRATEGY #1:

*Why are you here? What do you hope to gain or
accomplish from this book? What do you want your
recovery to look like one year from now?*

(Go to your Battle Strategy in the back of the book on
page 228 to answer.)

CHAPTER TWO >>

RECOGNIZING THE ENEMY

HOW WE GOT HERE

A basic part of training for any war is to know the enemy—inside and out. One big reason pornography keeps such a hold over us is that we get confused about what it actually is. Time to blow its cover.

In this chapter, we'll be breaking down what we're up against in a number of ways—starting with an exploration of how we got to this point as a society in the first place.

Compared to when your parents were growing up, things are very different today. So why have things changed? How did porn become so accepted and normal in our culture anyway? There are lots of reasons, but for now let's focus on four of the biggest contributors to how our culture became so pornified over the last several decades.

CONTRIBUTOR #1: WE DIDN'T KNOW ANY BETTER

This first contributor is something we've already spoken about plenty: a lack of knowledge. When we look back on our world's history and even our own personal history, we find that most of the time when we do something that is harmful to ourselves, it's because we just didn't know any better. Knowledge is often something that comes slowly and with time. As we discussed earlier, it was only recently that we started to discover that pornography was something that could be addictive and had harmful effects.

That was not something we had a whole lot of scientific evidence on thirty years ago. In fact, around that time one prominent person was arguing just the opposite, claiming that pornography was natural and even healthy. In 1948, Dr. Alfred Kinsey argued that all forms of sexual behavior should be normalized and that people should pursue their sexual urges no matter how young or old the person was.

At about the same time, one businessman took advantage of this same lack of knowledge and a magazine called *Playboy* started hitting the newsstands. *Playboy* attempted to present pornography as something respectable by marketing itself as a men's lifestyle magazine with renowned journalists writing articles on topics ranging from politics to sports to fashion, which appeared alongside pornographic images.

Because of this marketing tactic, the magazine's acceptance grew and paved the way for other publications to follow suit. Since then, thousands of magazines, film producers, and marketers have joined together to form an industry that today makes four times more money than the NBA, NFL, NHL, and MLB combined. Would all this have happened if the public had been aware of the true effects of pornography on individuals and relationships? No way!

Because of the overall lack of education and awareness on the true effects of pornography, we have allowed our society to become engulfed in a sexually hijacked culture.

CONTRIBUTOR #2: CRAZY-AWESOME TECHNOLOGY

Pornography has been around for a long time. It has shown up on cave walls, on ancient Greek pottery, and in medieval paintings. For most of human history, however, up to our parents' generation, pornography was something you had to do some work to find. You either had to go somewhere or buy something. It certainly wasn't in everyone's face.

All that started to change about forty years ago, with the creation of VHS tapes in 1971. Do you remember

VHS tapes? They're those giant black cassette tapes that play movies. The invention of VHS tapes made it possible for the first time for people to bring movies into their own homes. As a result, video rental stores opened everywhere—many of them with a "back room" for pornographic rentals.

And just like that, pornographic movies were suddenly showing up at home. DVDs soon replaced VHS tapes, and public acceptance of pornography continued to expand. Then came the Internet in 1993—an invention that changed the game forever. The Internet has influenced nearly every aspect of our lives today—with benefits that are obvious. Unfortunately, this invention has also multiplied the prevalence of pornography in our society exponentially.

Almost overnight pornography became available to anybody with an Internet connection. It could be accessed without ever leaving home; people didn't even have to rent anything. Today many of you are walking around with some kind of Internet-enabled mobile device, such as a laptop, smartphone, or tablet. Did your parents have those things growing up? Not even close.

At that time, if someone wanted access to pornographic material they had to go out and find it, and in most cases the fear of getting caught was enough for them to keep their addiction at bay. For you, all the best and worst of the universe is just a few clicks away. Ain't technology great?

CONTRIBUTOR #3: THE ALMIGHTY DOLLAR

Technology alone, of course, is not responsible for our pornified culture. At its most basic level, the media is just a messenger—neither positive nor negative in itself. As you know, technology can be used in many ways and for many reasons.

And one of those reasons is this: making money. Once that becomes the top goal of those producing media, guess what? Anything that makes more money is fair game—even if it hurts people. And sure enough, it didn't take long for someone to try using sex to make more money.

The earliest known use of pornography in advertising was by the Pearl Tobacco brand in 1871, when the company featured a naked woman on the package cover.Another example is Woodbury's Facial Soap, a woman's beauty bar. This soap was almost taken off the shelves in 1910 because nobody was buying it. The company gave one last attempt to increase sales by releasing an ad for the product that contained images of romantic couples and promises of love and intimacy for those using the brand (Sivulka, 1997). Guess what happened after they did that? Yep, their sales shot up significantly and they decided to keep the product on the shelves. Over the years, advertising companies have continued to find that sexuality is an effective way to increase a company's bottom line. Why do you think that is?

To answer that question, let's think back to the brain science of addiction. As with drugs or alcohol, remember that high levels of chemicals are released into the reward pathway when someone is viewing pornography. That chemical flood starts not from injecting or inhaling anything—but instead, from simply taking images in through the eyes. Without knowing it, the media acts as this drug's distributor. And all an advertiser or TV producer has to do to get those addictive chemicals pumping in your brain is show a little skin.

As soon as media producers and advertising agencies realized that "sex sells," it changed everything. Today, they continue to push closer and closer toward full-blown pornography because they know it will likely mean more dollars in their pockets. Anyone else a little irritated?

CONTRIBUTOR #4: THINGS TAKE TIME

So with all the new research, what's taking so long for things to change? As a final factor in where we are today, we need to talk about one more pattern: cultural change happens extremely slow. First, science has to catch up with truth; then, societies' behaviors have to catch up with science. Bottom line: things don't change quickly.

Tobacco, once again, provides a helpful illustration. People have been smoking for thousands of years. And for almost that long, most were convinced that it was harmless—or even good for them. It wasn't until 1938 that Dr. Raymond Pearl discovered that smoking tobacco could cause lung cancer. And what do you think happened next? Did society immediately reject tobacco and build statues of Dr. Pearl, thanking him for a discovery that could save millions of lives? Nope.

In fact, very few people even heard about him because the massive tobacco industry silenced his research and prevented it from going public. Not until nearly 15 years later, after Dr. Pearl had passed away, did his research see the light of day when *Reader's Digest* published an article titled "Cancer by the Carton." That forced a public debate that eventually turned into a lawsuit that found its way to the Supreme Court, where the tobacco industry testified under oath that their product was in no way addictive.

Hundreds of millions of dollars were spent on both sides of this battle, which lasted forty years! Today, there isn't anybody around who would argue that smoking tobacco is good for you. Smoking still exists, of course, but those who do it are pretty well informed on what it can lead to.

We're working for the same thing to happen with pornography. Over the last few decades, hard evidence has emerged that pornography can actually cause harm to our brains and our relationships. However, this doesn't mean that our culture will immediately change its attitudes and perceptions on the issue. It will take years—decades perhaps—to have a complete cultural shift.

Just as we look back and laugh at how we once thought smoking was good for you, one day your kids will look back on this time and say, "Remember how we thought pornography was harmless? Yeah, that was crazy." At least you're ahead of the curve!

So there you have it: ignorance, technology, money and time. Now that we've reviewed these four contributors, let's talk a little about pornography itself.

SYNTHETIC SEXUALITY: WHAT PORN REALLY IS

When people find out that you're actually trying to quit pornography for good, you'll probably hear something like this: "Watching porn is just expressing a natural drive!" or "Suppressing these sexual urges is unhealthy!" Have you heard something like that before?

It's not a new idea. Nearly a hundred years ago, Freud was saying the same kind of thing. Fifty years later, that Kinsey guy we mentioned was pushing the idea that all sexual urges should be followed. Because the body has a built-in appetite for sex, the argument goes, pornography use is natural and normal. Is that true?

What would you think if we told you that eating Twinkies is simply reflecting a natural drive that should not be resisted because the body has a built-in appetite for food?

What do you think about that? The food industry has figured out that by combining certain ingredients (especially sugar, fat, and salt), they can trigger a huge chemical rush in your body and produce a dopamine punch to the cranium—enough to make us feel our body needs and wants it.

In fact, one researcher spent a whole year tracking down every ingredient that went into the Twinkie—*all thirty-nine of them*. They include the preservative ascorbic acid (derived from natural gas), artificial colors, and flavorings formulated from petroleum. Cellulose gum, Polysorbate 60, and calcium sulfate are also ingredients—these are also used in sheet rock, shampoo, and rocket fuel. And it's limestone that makes Twinkies lightweight. That's right, there are skeletons of marine microorganisms and coral in every bite.

Bottom line, while the Twinkie is a finely crafted product that packs a punch in its taste, it is only barely a food—with almost no nutritional value of any kind.

Are you seeing the pornography comparison here? Stay with us: Have you ever wondered why you sometimes feel uneasy after eating junk food? Although the body may get an initial buzz off this food, the product has been so significantly altered from its natural form that your body has a difficult time recognizing it as food. When substances are that unnatural, your body can actually switch into attack mode where white blood cells fight the "food" you eat as an invading enemy!

How does this apply to pornography? Like an appetite for food, sexual feelings are of course a normal part of physiology. When two people come together in a real sexual relationship, giving themselves to each other fully, the intensity of pleasure is powerful. That is natural and normal.

What isn't normal is the complex system that different industries have developed to capitalize off our sexual appetite. The same way smokers get hooked on cigarettes, when we take the pornographic bait, our bodies get a buzz from a finely crafted product—one designed to maximize an immediate rush of pleasure. And yet, have you ever wondered why a dose of pornography sometimes leaves you empty or sickened?

In pornography, healthy sexuality has been cut from its original form, soaked, filtered, boiled, synthesized, and wholly exaggerated, all with an aim of creating the biggest chemical rush possible in your system. That is why we talk about porn being a drug. Can you see how something destructive might actually feel like a positive experience?

Now, when we say "pornography" in this discussion, recognize that there are many forms of synthetic sexuality. Pornography can be visual (pictures or videos), it can be written (blogs, books, or articles), and it can even appear in music. It can also be interactive, such as online chatting or talking over the phone. What unites all of these is the fact that they're all a form of artificially enhanced sexual stimulation. Just as Twinkies are an artificially enhanced and modified food that really isn't good for you, pornography is an artificially enhanced and modified sexual experience that isn't good for you either, and your body and mind both know it.

This should help if you ever start to wonder, "What's the difference between the experience of a healthy sexual relationship with a partner and the sexual experience of pornography? They're both sexual, so it's just two kinds of the same thing, right?"

Are they?

Not even close. It's a pretty good question. Like Twinkies and whole grain bread, while they may look similar from the outside, they result in very different experiences. Imagine for a moment being lost in a blistering desert. After two days of wandering without any food or water, you come across an abandoned village on the beach of what seems to be the ocean. Your attention immediately focuses on the massive body of salt water crashing on the coast only a few hundred meters ahead. In the corner of your eye you also notice a fresh water pump next to the nearest structure in the abandoned village, but all you can think about is drinking that cold ocean water. You think to yourself, "Water is water, isn't it? Whether I get it from the ocean or find it in the village doesn't really matter, right?"

Actually it does. You see, what you might not know is that drinking that salt water would kill you faster than if you didn't drink any water at all. Even though fresh water and salt water look nearly identical, their effects couldn't be more opposite. One replenishes and strengthens your body, and the other harms your body. In a similar way, sexuality is expressed in many forms—forms that can look similar from the outside. Depending on the details, however, they can have totally different effects.

So what are those details that make such a difference? Let's start with the biggest: the presence of another actual person. In a pornographic sexual experience, rather than interacting with another human being, your physiological system is being manipulated to respond to an image, with the body provoked by someone who is not really there. As this happens, your brain releases oxytocin, which is referred to as the "bonding chemical." This chemical is meant to create a sense of connection or bond between two loving individuals. In a pornographic experience, however, that chemical is being released in association with a hollow image behind a computer screen or on a magazine page. That is pretty confusing to the brain and over time your ability to bond with another real, actual person weakens.

Basically, pornography is a counterfeit—a lie. What it teaches you about sex and those you are attracted to is not only false but in many cases it's also destructive. It won't bring you a sense of connection, acceptance, or love. It won't vitalize or strengthen a relationship. It will slowly change your perceptions of women and men and distort your ideas of what a healthy sexual relationship should look like.

WHAT ARE THE EFFECTS OF PORNOGRAPHY ANYWAY?

We've said a lot so far about the research showing the true effects of pornography. In spite of this, people still sometimes laugh and joke at the idea that pornography could become a harmful addiction. They might say, "Oh come on, I've never seen anyone's teeth fall out because of a pornography addiction. So what's the big deal?"

So let's talk about it and get specific. After hundreds of studies, it's clear that pornography has some serious effects on the brain and on our relationships.

The United States Congress asked Dr. Jill Manning, a therapist who has worked with hundreds of pornography addicts, to review the research on pornography's effects and share what she found. In a special congressional hearing in November 2005, Dr. Manning shared a report detailing several areas of harm:

First of all, there is clear evidence that long-term pornography use sets people up for feeling more depressed and empty than those who do not use it. One big reason for this is that the pleasure center in the brain gets so worn out by constant artificial stimulation that it simply stops being able to respond to more natural kinds of pleasure.

Over time, users slowly start to become numb or desensitized to everyday activities. Plain and simple, life can start to feel pretty dull when we're exposing ourselves to unnatural levels of artificial stimulation all of the time. Everything else can eventually become as boring and bland as an hour-long infomercial about tube socks.

One of the scariest effects of extended pornography use is how it starts to change our experiences with other people. On a broad level, pornography use can cause people to feel less interested in caring about others around them.

What about romantic partners? One of the things many people look forward to most in life is a relationship, an exciting romance with satisfying sexual experiences. Some people believe that pornography helps to improve our sexuality and make romance even more exciting.

Studies actually show the opposite is true: pornography creates less closeness between partners, less excitement romantically, and less satisfaction in real sexual experiences (Zillmann & Bryant, 1988). Not only that, but it also actually increases the user's appetite for more porn. It's almost like we can't be satisfied once we develop this kind of appetite—we're always seeking for more. Researchers at Dartmouth's social health psychology lab discovered that "racy scenes" in movies and TV shows also lead to sex at an earlier age with more casual partners and more unsafe sex (Peng, 2012). If racy scenes on television are negatively influencing us, then just imagine the effect hard-core pornography has.

Unfortunately, there are also more serious problems that breed from pornography addiction, such as having completely unrealistic expectations about sexual partners. Researchers have found that after being exposed to pornography, subjects were less satisfied with their partners' affection, physical appearance, sexual curiosity, and sexual performance (Zillmann & Bryant, 1988).

A friend of ours named Maria told us that after she was newly married she and her husband started looking at pornography together to spice up their love life. After a while they started looking at pornography on their own, and over time they ended up preferring the computer screen to the real thing. Eventually her marriage fell apart. She was able to recover, but her ex-husband never did.

Unfortunately, Maria is not alone. This is an epidemic that is sweeping across developed countries and harmfully impacting families and relationships. Research indicates 56 percent of all divorces in the US involved at least one party having an "obsessive interest in pornographic websites" (Fagan, 2009).

Another harmful effect of pornography is that it has caused many individuals to become uncomfortable with real bodies and think that the photoshopped images and unrealistic videos they've been exposed to are what they should expect.

One counselor called this problem Sexual Attention Deficit Disorder, saying, "Just as people with real ADD tend to be easily distracted, guys with SADD have become so accustomed to the high levels of visual novelty and stimulation ... that they're unable to focus on ... a real woman" (Kerner, 2011). And guess what: the same thing goes for women. They begin to compare their sex lives to what they see as much more glamorous and arousing on screen.

Therapist Susan Orbach writes of an "eroding individual appreciation of the unaltered human form." Another researcher summarized her findings from hundreds of interviews by saying that individuals are developing "a distorted sense of what a normal woman's body is," adding, "suddenly a normal woman's body looks abnormal" (Hamilton, 2009).

In addition to distorting perceptions, expectations of sexuality, relationships, and the appearance of partners, the FBI's statistics show that pornography is found at 80% of the scenes of violent sex crimes or in the homes of the perpetrators (Anderson, 1992).

But let's go back to where the rubber hits the road for all of us: our relationships. And not just any relationships, but the ones we care about most.

Research shows that pornography leads people to care less about committing to anyone for very long—especially with marriage. Statistics show that if they do get married, individuals with pornography problems are more likely to have tension with their partner, to have less interest in having children, and to pay less attention to the children that are born; they also have an increased likelihood of cheating, separation, and divorce (Zillman & Bryant, 1984 & 1988 and Daines & Shumway, 2011). Oh good ol' pornography—supporting family values since... never.

Don't get discouraged, though. The opposite pattern is also true. Individuals who leave pornography behind and cultivate a healthy perception of what bodies should look like are significantly more likely to be involved in a committed, healthy relationship. As we said at the beginning, today can be a new day for any one of us.

QUICK QUESTION:
What are the effects of pornography that you've seen in your own life?

THE INDUSTRY'S DIRTY LITTLE SECRET

Before diving into exploring your own situation, we need to talk about something pretty serious—one more facet of this industry that is aiming to make you a life-long customer. To those of us who end up watching it, pornography can appear to be a fantasy world of pleasure and thrills. The experiences of those who create and participate in making pornography, however, are often flooded with drugs, disease, rape, and abuse. It's easy to be unaware of all the shady details that go on behind the scenes. The pornography industry wants to keep it that way—as secretive as possible. Fortunately, more and more former porn stars are speaking up. For example:

> I got the *&%$ kicked out of me ... most of the girls start crying because they're hurting so bad ... I couldn't breathe. I was being hit and choked. I was really upset and they didn't stop. They kept filming. [I asked them to turn the camera off] and they kept going. —Regan, former porn industry worker

In order to prevent the police and the public from finding out about the conditions pornography is created under, it's common for pornographers to intimidate or use blackmail as a weapon to silence the participants. Many former porn stars talk about being booked to do a scene only to have conditions changed on the spot, which often led to uncomfortable, abusive experiences. In a very real way, then, porn stars get treated like convenient cattle. They are lied to by the industry's "doctors" about the prevalence of sexually transmitted diseases (STDs) and many abuse drugs to cope with their emotionally deteriorating lives. Another actor said:

> You're viewed as an object and not as a human with a spirit. People don't care. People do drugs because they can't deal with the way they are being treated ... Seventy-five percent [of porn stars] ... are using drugs. They have to numb themselves. There are specific doctors in this industry that if you

go in for a common cold they'll give you Vicodin, Viagra,
anything you want because all they care about is the money.
You are a number ... You have to numb yourself to go on set.
The more you work, the more you have to numb yourself.
—Jersey, former porn industry worker

Working in pornography isn't the dream job that pornographers want people to believe it is. And yet because
the industry is legally recognized by the government, it
comes with a false sense of security. In addition to keeping people quiet, doctors are employed by the industry to
"watch over" the actors and actresses. Because these doctors are paid to support the pornographers, they don't act
to protect their patients, and STD's remain a huge problem in the industry.

When I was in the industry, the fear of bodily fluids ... was
absolutely disregarded ... There is no protection or hygiene
at all. We weren't allowed to use condoms. The constant
spreading of germs and disease-ridden materials is not even
considered by the employees of the production companies
... [Props, furniture, cleaning towels, etc.] are not thorough-
ly sanitized or sterilized. That is unsanitary and completely
unsafe. —Trent, former porn industry worker

OK, so we have rape, coercion, and preventable diseases.
What else happens? Sex trafficking (a.k.a., modern slavery for sexual purposes), that's what. You might be thinking, "Wait, that really happens?" Sadly, yes. Sex trafficking is a $32 billion per year industry. According to the
U.N., more than 9.7 million people around the world are
ensnared in sex slavery at any given time—including
young boys and girls. Guess what the majority of those
individuals are forced into doing? You guessed it: porn.
Their lives are threatened if they don't make it look like
they are enjoying what they are doing. That means the
millions of people who think they are viewing "harmless
porn" are often literally watching someone being forced
against their will to participate in sexual acts.

I literally became a prisoner. I was not allowed out of his sight, not even to use the bathroom, where he watched me through a hole in the door. He slept on top of me at night. He listened to my telephone calls with a .45 automatic eight shot pointed at me. —Linda, former porn industry worker

It's hard to imagine, but could it get any worse? Unfortunately, it can and does. One actress was reported missing after a film session. A month later she was found with multiple stab wounds—with DNA evidence tying the murder to her photographer. Some might think, "That kind of thing happens all over, not just in the pornography industry." That's true. However, these stories and testimonies from ex–porn stars are surfacing more and more. Some that have escaped have even dedicated their lives to speaking out against the industry, such as Shelly Lubben, Elizabeth Rollings, and Danielle Williams.

At Fight the New Drug we have received several direct emails from former porn stars telling us their stories. Nearly all of them ask that we keep their identity secret for fear of being harmed by their former employers. Here is an example of one of those emails:

I speak from experience to say there are victims and survivors who have been drugged and forced into this ugliness against their wills. I realize that this statement flies in the face of the mainstream stereotypical mono-thought mentality that porn is voluntary and that "she likes it," "she asked for it," "she chose it." Although that may be true for some, many are coerced into agreeing with whatever our pornographer says just to stay alive. We have been humiliated beyond description and carry that with us 24/7. Our minds are numbed and in many cases drugged into stupor or amnesia for the painful tearing at our bodies and souls just to be filmed, forever recorded for someone's sick fantasy to come alive for momentary gratification.

I was drugged before each filming. Sometimes it was with an amnesiac, sometimes with a paralyzing drug, sometimes with pain blockers, and sometimes a crazy combination of all of the above.

We lie to cover up the truth much the same way the victim of domestic abuse lies, conceals, and hides. We do not have the words to speak out because our pain is too graphic and it is next to impossible to describe what happened to us because of the mainstream mentality. We are met with dismissals and denials, with excuses [such as], "that could not have happened, because the girls and women look like they enjoy what is happening to them."

Some of us have succumbed to more drug addictions, some to insanity, some to crippling isolation, and some to death.

Wow. Doesn't that leave you a little sick to your stomach? Not only does pornography have harmful effects on the user, but the industry itself and those that participate in it deal with incredible harm to their bodies and overall lives.

Bottom line: The industry's efforts to portray an atmosphere of glamour, fame, and fortune have allowed them to get away with illegal, unethical, and corrupt behavior. In addition to all the personal reasons you have to rebel against this industry, keep in mind the reality of those being victimized every day. We don't have to stand for it, not anymore.

THE ADDICTION CYCLE

All right, Fighters. We know that last section was heavy, but knowing what you now know is a crucial part of understanding our enemy. Now it's time to get more specific on how exactly we're going to beat this thing.

The real reason you're here is that you want to get rid of this addiction. You've been trapped for far too long, spinning like dirty laundry, and you've had enough. We want to help you get out, and to do that, we need to first talk about what exactly it is that you're stuck in. Have you ever heard of the addiction cycle?

The addiction cycle is something you're probably familiar with, whether you realize it or not. That's because many of us have been gripped in its headlock for a long time. This cycle describes the pattern many of us get stuck in—a pattern that we're usually not entirely conscious of. In fact, one reason this addiction cycle has such a hold on us is that it usually goes undetected by our radars.

So, we're going to change that right now. By talking about the cycle openly, we're going to begin decreasing its power over all of us. Let's give you a visual to reference as we talk about it (see the next page).

THE ADDICTION CYCLE

At times, everyone feels sad, lonely, bored, angry, stressed, or over-whelmed. These feelings are normal and expected. It is very important to understand how to deal with these discomforts of life when they arise. Unhealthy decisions can lead to falling into the addiction cycle.

START

DISCOMFORTS OF LIFE

THESE DISCOMFORTS ARE NORMAL

WANTING RELIEF FROM THE DISCOMFORTS OF LIFE

ESCAPING THE

CHOOSE A HEALTHY RESPONSE TO THE DISCOMFORTS OF LIFE

HEALTHY RESPONSES

DISCOMFORTS DECREASE OVER TIME

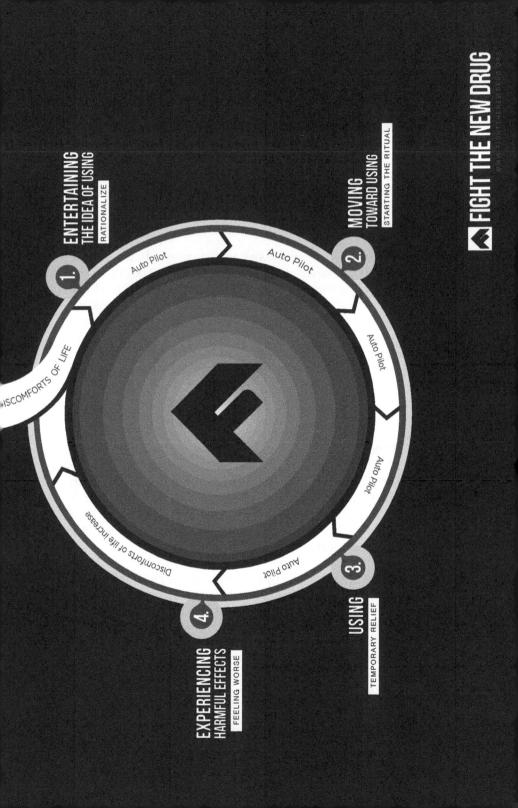

1. **ENTERTAINING**
THE IDEA OF USING
RATIONALIZE

2. **MOVING**
TOWARD USING
STARTING THE RITUAL

3. **USING**
TEMPORARY RELIEF

4. **EXPERIENCING**
HARMFUL EFFECTS
FEELING WORSE

Auto Pilot

Auto Pilot

Auto Pilot

Auto Pilot

Auto Pilot

DISCOMFORTS OF LIFE

Discomforts of life increase

Alright, let's dive in.

If you look up in the top left corner of the addiction cycle, you'll see "start." That's where we all begin. You'll notice above that there are several life problems that you are probably familiar with. These discomforts are normal and unavoidable—everybody has them to some degree or another. Stress, anxiety, pressure, boredom, and loneliness happen to all of us; and it's natural to want relief from these discomforts.

What pushes someone toward addiction is when we start to respond to these discomforts of life in one specific way: trying to escape them. What do we mean by that? Seeking relief, of course, can be a good thing. We're not talking about all the positive things you can do to relieve pain when you're hurting. We're talking about an extreme demand to *get rid* of any discomfort we are facing at any cost. For many people facing addiction, trying to find an immediate escape from these discomforts of life is a big reason they drink, smoke, do drugs—or use porn.

Scientific research has confirmed that trying to escape from discomfort lies at the heart of many addictions. After all, thinking we shouldn't *have* to feel what we're feeling, makes it easy to start thinking that we've got to find something to numb us out. It's at this point that it becomes easy to start to think about some Web site or a video that will bring immediate but temporary relief. We call this "entertaining the idea of using."

In most cases, this all happens without our realizing it—without us even being aware that this cycle is even going on and pulling us in. At this point, we have released the steering wheel and let autopilot drive the bus. It's something that we all do sometimes when we're distracted and not paying attention to what we're really thinking, feeling, or experiencing. Has that ever happened to you? Have you ever found yourself going through the motions without really thinking about the consequences? Before you know it, you've used again. When we're in autopilot mode, we often fall, robot-like, into vulnerable situations.

When this happens, our addiction is steering our actions, leading us to just go along with whatever our addiction wants. For drug users this could mean winding up under the bridge downtown where the dealers slum around, or hanging out with a user friend from their past.

With pornography, this could be booting up your computer when no one is around and locking the door. It could be wandering around a movie rental place or dilly-dallying down the magazine aisle of a bookstore. It is putting yourself in an environment in which you normally get exposed to pornography. We call this "moving toward using" or "starting the ritual."

Can you start to see yourself in this cycle at all? By recognizing what's happening, you'll be in a good place to learn how to step out of the cycle.

Let's keep going. You haven't stepped out of it this time. You are on autopilot, moving toward using. At this point, anticipation builds, your focus narrows, and resisting the urge to use seems impossible. So we give in. We "use," and get that temporary numbing feeling. Like another cigarette, another drink, or another food binge, a porn binge triggers a chemical rush in seconds.

Our emptiness, anxiety, or boredom is again covered up and relieved in some way. And for that moment, we have some distraction from whatever discomfort we were feeling. The problem is that soon, we feel even worse than we did before.

In the long-run the discomfort not only doesn't go away but also gets worse, because we haven't dealt with what the real problem is. But we're not usually paying attention to this. In fact, we can become so anxious about *not* feeling that discomfort that we don't care very much about the fact that we'll feel worse later on. We're calling that "experiencing harmful effects."

This is the ironic part of the cycle. As pornography becomes the primary solution to dealing with the discomforts of life, it can actually become the cause of stress rather than a relief from it. As "the discomforts of life increase," we can begin to use even more and more pornography to escape the increasing amount of pain and discomfort arising from the cycle.

And the next time life gets a little anxious, hard, or boring, we think again, "Why do I need to feel this way when I can have relief?" The cycle perpetuates, and we spiral downward as the harmful effects compound. Pretty soon, we're trapped inside something we didn't really want— an emotional cancer that is multiplying out of control, hijacking our freedom and our ability to live a healthy life.

So let's go through this with an example you might experience. Let's say that your parents left the house for a few hours and that you are home alone. For the first little while, you start working on some homework. After a while, you get to some hard assignments and feel yourself feeling uncomfortable and starting to get a little anxious. At this point, you have a choice, although you may not realize it: "Is it OK to feel some anxiety, or do I have to make it go away?" Your reaction is almost automatic. "I don't want to feel this. I've got to take a break to get some relief." Rather than being OK with a little anxiety and continuing your homework, you've just taken your first step into the cycle.

So you turn on the computer to surf around a bit. With no one else in the home, you realize that you could explore Web sites that you normally wouldn't if others were around. At first you resist, but the idea keeps coming back and pretty soon you start rationalizing: "I won't look at anything really bad." So you check again to make sure you are still alone. Before you know it, you've used again. After that, you feel empty, disappointed, or maybe even embarrassed. You think to yourself, "How on earth did I let that happen?!" Well, our answer is, "Dude, you just fell into the addiction cycle again!" Did you notice the other steps of the cycle we discussed? After taking that first step, it went boom, boom, boom: entertaining the idea of using, moving toward using, using, then experiencing the harmful effects and discomfort getting worse. We're usually not aware of these steps. But if we are, it can help us do something about them.

Now that you're aware of the addiction cycle, you probably realize something pretty cool—something that we talked about earlier: YOU ARE NOT YOUR ADDICTION. You now have a visual of the larger problem, and it's not just about you. You can finally separate yourself from your behaviors and start to look at your addiction in a new way. You now have a bird's eye view of the problem, and as you look around, you will begin noticing places throughout the addiction cycle where you can step out of it. These are called "choice points," and that's where we're heading next.

QUICK QUESTION:
What do you think of the addiction cycle we just finished describing? Can you find yourself in that cycle? Can you identify the specific discomforts of life that you may be trying to escape?

⊛ ACTION

Over the next week, try to notice your own experience with the addiction cycle. Recognize where you are in the cycle and take specific note of your thoughts and emotions. As simple as it sounds, being aware that you are entering a stage of the addiction cycle is essential to stepping out of it and moving toward freedom.

CHOICE POINTS: STEPPING OUT OF THE ADDICTION CYCLE

As the addiction cycle drags someone along toward using again, again, and again, it is understandable that he or she can feel a bit hopeless. After months and years of feeling dragged through the cycle, it can feel like there is no out. No options. No other way forward.

When you're in the middle of the cycle (especially when you're unaware that it's happening), let's admit it: that feels true. Like someone lost in a maze and not even realizing they're in a maze, there is little chance you're going to find your way out.

But what if you *did* realize you're in a maze or a cycle that's leading you in circles? What if someone handed you a map of these larger patterns and started showing you where you were going wrong, along with all the other paths available to you? Would that change things for you?

Here is some good news about the addiction cycle: there is a way out. Like a prison that seems impossible to escape, if you watch and listen carefully, there are places to chip away and finally to break out of it. These points of possible choice arise at different times and in moments that will surprise you. As you take advantage of these escape routes, you will be able to slip out of the addiction cycle and walk free.

Victor Frankl, a renowned therapist and Holocaust survivor, once said, "Between stimulus and response, there is a space. In that space is our power to choose our response, and in our response lies our growth and our freedom" (Frankl, 2006).

This may sound strange at first, but think about it. As an addiction becomes stronger, there seem to be no spaces at all. Like an old trail, the moments of choice become grown over, hidden, and seemingly impossible to find. And so we get lost. Ready to find the trail again?

Go ahead and look at the cycle again with the added choice points (see the next page). You'll notice that there are four main choice points throughout the cycle that give us the opportunity to step out and move in a new direction toward freedom. As we discussed earlier, the discomforts of life are something we all feel. No one is immune to this. It's a part of life.

However, like we said, it's all about how we respond to those discomforts that makes the difference of whether or not you go down into the addiction cycle or go in a better direction. On one hand, those that choose to respond to those discomforts in a healthy way avoid the cycle altogether. Instead of trying to just escape the discomforts, there are an infinite variety of things we can do in moments of discomfort to help us work with and move through those feelings: talking with friends, getting outside, reading something, and taking some quiet time are some examples. If you continue to respond in a healthy way, guess what: the discomforts of life can actually begin to decrease over time. They don't feel as heavy, and some of those discomforts can even go away for good.

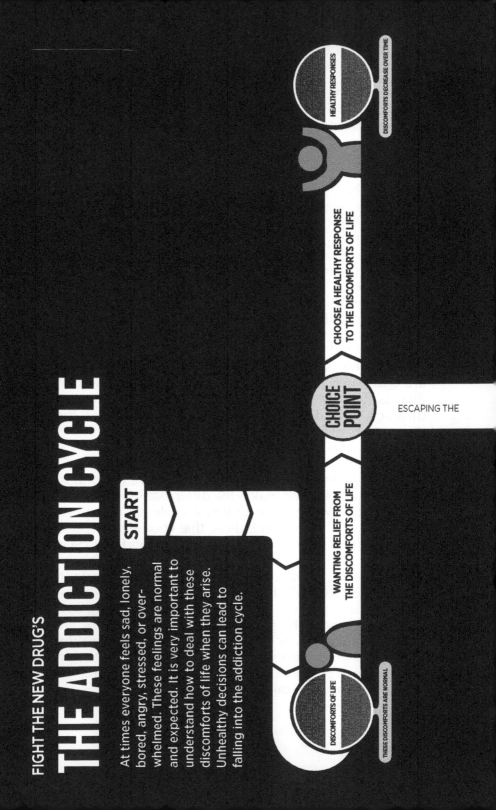

FIGHT THE NEW DRUG'S

THE ADDICTION CYCLE

At times everyone feels sad, lonely, bored, angry, stressed, or over-whelmed. These feelings are normal and expected. It is very important to understand how to deal with these discomforts of life when they arise. Unhealthy decisions can lead to falling into the addiction cycle.

START

WANTING RELIEF FROM
THE DISCOMFORTS OF LIFE

DISCOMFORTS OF LIFE

THESE DISCOMFORTS ARE NORMAL

CHOICE POINT

ESCAPING THE

CHOOSE A HEALTHY RESPONSE
TO THE DISCOMFORTS OF LIFE

HEALTHY RESPONSES

DISCOMFORTS DECREASE OVER TIME

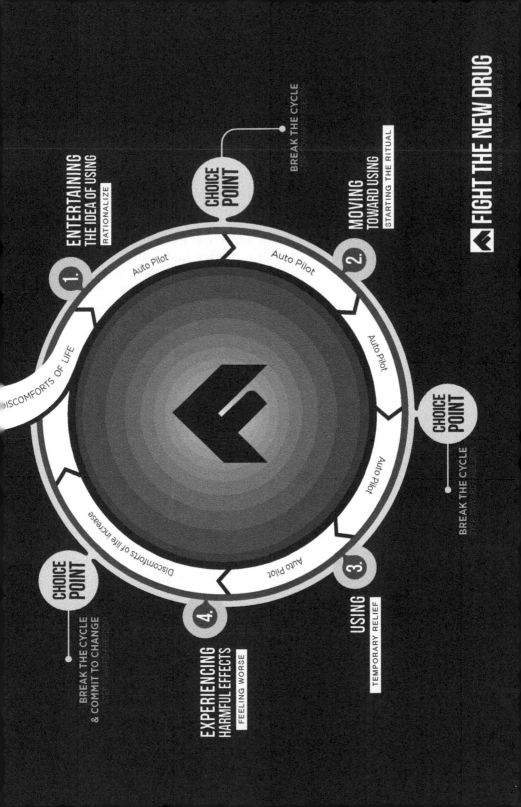

FIGHT THE NEW DRUG
WWW.FIGHTTHENEWDRUG.ORG

CHOICE POINT
BREAK THE CYCLE

CHOICE POINT
BREAK THE CYCLE

CHOICE POINT
BREAK THE CYCLE & COMMIT TO CHANGE
STEP TOWARD FREEDOM

1.
ENTERTAINING THE IDEA OF USING
RATIONALIZE

2.
MOVING TOWARD USING
STARTING THE RITUAL

3.
USING
TEMPORARY RELIEF

4.
EXPERIENCING HARMFUL EFFECTS
FEELING WORSE

Auto Pilot

Auto Pilot

Auto Pilot

Auto Pilot

Auto Pilot

Discomforts of life increase

DISCOMFORTS OF LIFE

On the other hand, if we try to escape, we're not focused on adjusting our lives in a way that gets to the root of the discomfort. Instead, we're focused on something else: making the discomfort go away—NOW. And there goes your first choice point. Do you really want to make that choice? Do you really have to focus your energy on escaping the discomfort immediately? Or are there some steps that are wiser, that will lead you to real and lasting relief?

Soon, we'll be talking about more details of what these healthier steps look like. For now, we just want to point out that a choice exists right where we weren't looking: between the moment of discomfort and the moment of deciding we have to escape. But do we really have to escape? Let's say we decide we do want to make the discomfort go away by escaping rather than facing it. What's next? You're feeling anxious, hungry, bored, tired, or sad, and you want a distraction. You've been trying to stay away from porn, but even so, you decide to get on the Internet—not to search for porn, of course, just to browse. Because you're anxious to get rid of the discomfort, though, this innocent browse takes a turn. You're on YouTube and a questionable thumbnail for a video down in the corner draws your eye. A thought comes, "Oh, it's not a big deal," or "This doesn't hurt anyone."

Have you ever said that to yourself? Remember, this addiction cycle is powerful. It can sway our will power and fool us. At that moment, if you don't see what's going on and step away, even more rationalizations will kick in: "You know everyone's into this. Don't be such a prude— so old-fashioned. No one is going to find out about this. This is going to be totally fun. You can always stop later!"

If you are paying attention, you will recognize the moment all this propaganda starts hitting you as a second choice point—another chance to escape from this miserable cycle. So what do we mean? In the past, it's understandable if you've done what many do—accepting the rationalizations and following them as if they were real-ity. But what if you saw them differently—what if you saw them as a programmed script that is being fed to you, a script you can notice and reject? We'll say more about that soon. For now, just realize that you just discovered another moment to take control, another place where you don't have to be blindsided by the enemy anymore.

You've already got two moments where you can step away from the cycle. If you choose not to take those turns, then naturally you will end up moving toward using. Now you're closing the curtains and adjusting the computer's volume. Now there's no turning back—or is there?

Actually, it's not too late. It's never too late to step away. Right before using, you still have a choice to ask yourself, "Is this what I really want?" As you begin to pay closer attention to your experiences, you can pinpoint where you are in the cycle and notice the choice points all along the way. It's never too late to catch yourself and step away. And that includes the moment after you've started to use. When that happens, you might be tempted to think, "There, now you've blown it; no use holding back any more. You've done it again." Watch those thoughts. Notice how you feel. Is this really what you want to do? Do you really have to continue?

Even if you feel that temporary relief, do you feel better deep down? Maybe for a second, but then what happens? You feel worse. Feeling worse could be a wide range of things, from guilt, less satisfaction in relationships, stress in relationships due to use, etc., as the discomforts of life increase. Even after using, there are other choice points available: "Do I have to keep going for a long time? Can I stop sooner?" Even after using, you can realize, "I'm bet-ter than this!"

The earlier you respond in the cycle, of course, the easier

it will be to take that step toward freedom and move in the direction that you really want to go. But setbacks happen, and once they do, we need to learn from them. We can learn to see the kinds of conditions that set the stage for a setback and learn how to adjust and avoid them.

As you practice this skill of watching your experience carefully and recognizing choice points, you will find yourself gaining more and more strength—strength to not be dragged around anymore; strength to do what you really want and not be forced against your will. You may even be able to prevent some battles entirely.

It's important to realize, of course, that just because we start to notice choice points, that doesn't suddenly make things easy. You've likely been doing this long enough that your brain has been hardwired to act in a certain way. And those habits aren't going to change overnight.

In the next two sections we're going to give you an awesome tool to help get your brain in gear. First, though, let's go over some strategies for working with thoughts when they get a little crazy.

THINKING ABOUT THINKING

Have you ever wanted to shut off your thoughts? When facing an addiction, it's normal to have thoughts that hit us rapid-fire, pushing us one way or another—and making us feel a little controlled. Is there anything we can do in those moments?

Of course it's easiest in the short term to simply give into the thoughts and let them carry us wherever they are going. We all know where that leads. The only other option seems to be trying to control and manage these thoughts by trying to force them away. Ever tried this? While this can work for a short time, it can wear us out in the long-term.

So is there another way? What can we do instead? How about this: *watch your thoughts.*

Instead of trying to control thoughts we don't like by forcing them away, try watching them instead—sort of like you'd watch an interesting movie or like a scientist would watch an experiment.

As you try watching your thoughts, you will discover something interesting: thoughts can come and go on their own, like waves in the sea; and they sometimes change on their own, like weather patterns. The brain is constantly producing thoughts to help us make sense of the world. Over time, you can come to see these thoughts for what they are: just thoughts, rather than reality or who you are. In other words, you can come to see that *you are not your thoughts.*

As you begin to relate to your own thoughts in this way, you can begin to develop a cool skill: watching your mind without getting pulled into the action: "Oh, there's that rationalization coming up again. Here comes that propaganda again." In this way, you can learn to observe your thoughts, without blindly following them and without having to act on them. The same is true of feelings.

While it might sound strange, don't worry: this skill is very learnable, provided you're willing to work at it a little. The first time you practice watching your thoughts, you may be surprised at how hard it is—and at how crazy thoughts can be. One person described her thoughts as "kind of like wild monkeys, swinging around from tree to tree all over the place." Can you relate? With some practice, over time you will notice thoughts starting to behave themselves and calm down a bit, but in the meantime, you might have to be patient with some wild monkeys.

So here is the skill, in very simple form: Practice *watching* thought, rather than *being* thought. Practice *watch-*

ing feeling, rather than *being* feeling and living every feeling out. It's definitely not easy at first, but the more you do it, the better you'll become. And depending on how you respond to thoughts, you can gain more or less control over them. In the next chapter, we'll give you some awesome tools that will help you get this skill down like a pro!

QUICK QUESTION:
Have you ever thought about approaching your thoughts in this way? What do you think it could mean for your personal power in overcoming this addiction?

⭐ ACTION:

What we invite you to do today is practice watching thought, rather than being thought. Practice watching feeling, rather than being feeling. Take some time to enjoy a "thought parade" of your own. To do that, think of your thoughts and feelings as being in a parade—a parade you can choose to step out of and simply watch pass by rather than getting tangled up in whatever comes along. Whenever you find yourself having a barrage of thoughts, practice what we've talked about by stepping outside of them and watching them come by. See if you can do the same for feelings. Do you get pulled back into the parade? If so, can you catch yourself and step back out onto the sidewalk again?

CHAPTER THREE >> BASIC TRAINING

Welcome to basic training! Are you ready? Let's do this. Don't worry, no one is going to ask you to do push-ups.

We will be asking you to do other exercises, though—things that will probably stretch your mental muscles in new ways.

We won't try mastering everything at once. Instead, we'll take one step at a time—focusing on each of the core areas you may need to beat this addiction and achieve lasting change.

STRATEGY #1: S.T.A.R., PART I

Now that we are more aware of the addiction cycle and some of its hidden choice points, we realize there are multiple moments where we have the option to step out and move in a positive direction toward freedom. While this may sound simple, remember: it is not for wimps. Because we are so incredibly accustomed to autopilot, we can go about much of our lives only dimly aware of what we are doing. Moving in another direction—going against this sheer momentum—can be daunting.

In this section we're going to give you a tool to help ground and stabilize you when that urge to use pornography comes around. If you continue to pull out this ninja tool each time an urge arises, you will find yourself getting stronger with each battle and leaving those fights with fewer scars.

You ready for this? We call it S.T.A.R., which stands for:
    S – Step back and observe
    T – Take a few conscious breaths
    A – Ask yourself what you really want
    R – Respond in a healthy way

In olden times, when people were lost at sea they would look to the North Star for guidance—a fixed point that could help them find the right direction. In a similar way, this star can help to anchor us when we're feeling especially vulnerable and starting to get pulled back into the addiction cycle.

To begin, let's talk about the S in S.T.A.R.: step back and observe. As the urge to use is coming up inside of you, it can be helpful to step back, calmly observe the situation, and thoughtfully recognize what is really happening: "What am I really feeling here? What kinds of thoughts are hitting me? How does my body feel right now?" If we can do that one small step successfully, our chance of breaking the cycle and moving toward freedom has already grown enormously. This will take practice, and it won't be easy. But give it a try sometime. Wherever you are, whatever you're doing, start practicing now. And whenever that urge comes, stop and take a step back.

Taking a step back doesn't guarantee that we'll break the cycle. If we don't follow that step with something else, we'll likely just fall right back into autopilot and continue down the path of addiction. So let's talk about the rest of S.T.A.R.

Even after stepping back and observing the situation, it's easy to still feel unstable and pulled by the urge. Because of that, this next step is important: take a few slow, conscious breaths. This allows you to focus your thoughts and settle your mind. Close your eyes and notice your lungs fill up with air slowly, and then release. For thousands of years, people have been using breathing exercises as a way to ground themselves in the face of tough challenges. Brain scientists are discovering that something as simple as mindful breathing can help calm your body and mind by short-circuiting the charging chemical rush to your brain.

At this point, what you end up doing is still your choice, of course. But if you make the choice from a more settled place, you're more likely to do what you really want. And that leads to the next step—the A in S.T.A.R.: ask yourself what you really want. This will help you tune in to your true desires—what you really want and really hope for in the long run. Rather than just following whatever impulse hits your body at any given moment, give yourself a chance to tune in to your core values and sense what you want deep down. Once you've oriented yourself to what you really want, you will be better able to respond in a way that is in line with whatever your true desires are. But that doesn't mean the decision is settled.

It's still up to you to respond according to what you really want. The last step to S.T.A.R., then, is to respond in a healthy way and make a decision about what you are going to do. That means it's your choice: using or not. We're not here to control your choices. That's not our agenda. Instead, our agenda is to make sure your choices are really your choices and not just the instant impulse of the body or the momentum of an out-of-control cycle. And one way we're helping you move in this direction is by teaching you S.T.A.R.

By stepping back, taking a breath, and asking yourself what you really want, you're no longer driven to have an automatic reaction. Instead, you're in a position to make an authentic choice—a decision true to what you really want. Does that mean you could choose to use? Yes it does. However, the fact that you're in this program says a lot about what you really want.

As you access that place of calm, we don't think feeding a pornography addiction will be what you choose, at least not for long. Like others, you will probably begin to find that the deeper part of you doesn't really want to use as much as you thought. It wants something far more than porn could ever offer.

At the point where you are making your decision, it can be helpful to turn to another activity and replace the urge with something better.

Like what? Well, telling you to replace the urge with something better is easier said than done. Simply turning the page of the magazine or flipping to the next channel on television won't cut it. You're going to need something powerful to replace it if you're actually going to be able to overpower that chemical rush that started in your brain.

This is where your passions come in. Passions are things that you truly love doing or pursuing. It's more than just liking something. No, this goes much deeper than that. Passions are things we can hardly live without—things that make us who we are. These can include sports, mastering a musical instrument, spending time in the mountains, dancing, writing in your journal, blogging, or taking apart and rebuilding computers. Whatever your passions are, these are the things that are powerful enough to compete with and beat an urge.

Our suggestion is to keep a list of your passions close at hand. Whenever an urge shows up, you can take that list out and see which one is most realistic to pursue at that moment. You may also want to have a few passions that you can accomplish at any time, regardless of where you are and what hour of day it is, such as writing, art, personal exercise, or music. That way, if an urge hits at midnight, you don't have to try to call your buddies to organize a pickup game of basketball.

We've found that activities with physical exertion, such as playing sports, running, or going on a hike, have an incredible ability to reset the prefrontal cortex in the brain, which is where decisions are made. It's like hitting the restart button. If you've replaced the urge and it is still bothering you, it can be good to add the company of others for a while to provide a distraction and further motivate you not to use.

What if you're not sure if you have any passions? That's OK. Sometimes it takes time and experience to stumble across the things that you feel passionate about. Be patient and keep trying new things, and we promise that sooner or later you will find an activity, hobby, or idea that will be more powerful than an urge.

So what do you say? Are you ready to try this out? Let's say you're checking your email and you accidentally click on a link that immediately takes you to a pornographic Web site. You're shocked and quickly close the browser. You try and forget what you saw, but it's too late. Those images have triggered a release of chemicals into your brain and you start to feel a powerful urge coming on. This is the perfect opportunity to use S.T.A.R.

So you step back and observe what's really going on. You

take a few conscious breaths to soothe the wave of emotions and to regain control. Then you ask yourself what it
is you really want—truly and not just in that moment. As
you do so, you remember that giving in now will only be
temporarily satisfying—and definitely won't make you
feel more fulfilled in the long run. At this point, we're not
out of the woods yet, but you do feel just a little more
in control as you make a very important decision: what
to do next. This is the moment where we can either fall
back into the addiction cycle or choose to respond to the
urge by replacing it with something better—one of your
passions. After a short struggle, you choose to leave your
room and get outside to go hang out with friends.

Congratulations! You just won a battle!

At first glance, some might mistake S.T.A.R. as a simple
willpower bench press: "Alright, no problem, just choose
to turn away. That's easy!"

Please understand: that's not what we're saying. Remember, getting out of your addiction isn't simply a matter of
trying harder. Instead, it's a matter of fighting smart.

And that's the whole point of S.T.A.R.—four steps to help
ground you and interrupt the autopilot of the addiction
cycle, helping you tune in to what you really want. Notice
that there are four steps, rather than just "Choose something different!" We've also seen that if you just skip to
the last step, you'll miss the full impact of S.T.A.R. Be
sure to slow the process down and spend as much time as
needed on each step.

As you practice S.T.A.R., you will come out the other end
more aware of the choices you want to be making—rather
than defaulting to autopilot. Although this skill can support
a healthy response, that won't make it suddenly easy. Practicing this skill will take some real work. And moving in new
directions still takes great courage, effort, and dedication.

BATTLE STRATEGY #2:

Create your own list of passions or things that you absolutely love doing, so that you'll have plenty of options when the next urge hits. You can also write those passions down on a small piece of paper and carry the list with you in your pocket or wallet. Everybody is going to have different passions that work for them, so make it your own.

(Go to your Battle Strategy in the back of the book on page 228 to answer.)

⭐ ACTION

Go work on or participate in one of your passions right now. Pay attention to what it feels like to be doing something you truly love.

S.T.A.R., PART II

With what you've learned so far, you're prepared to fight smart. And if every urge went away when we turned to one of our passions, we'd be set.

We all know, however, that urges can sometimes follow you around and chomp at your heels like a pesky puppy. Urges can be stubborn, especially if you've been using for a while.

So to combat that, let's talk a little more about the R in S.T.A.R.: respond in a healthy way. We've already talked about one powerful way to respond, and that is to replace the urge with something better—one of your passions. While responding in this way can often be enough to help you during a battle, there is another way to respond that can be powerful when the urge doesn't seem to be going away.

Instead of turning away from the urge, try something brave: make eye contact with it. Hold your position with your feet firmly planted on the ground. Calmly observe what you are feeling and thinking. Try to stay curious, present, and calm as you watch the urge. Step back and observe your experience like we discussed doing with thoughts: as if you were watching a sporting event on TV. Notice how the urge changes and moves over time, like a wave in the ocean.

Once an urge begins and you feel the desire to use, most people generally believe that the craving will continue to increase in intensity until they give in to it. Isn't that how we usually think? From this perspective, an urge is a straight line that will continue to increase upward in intensity until we act on it or stop it somehow.

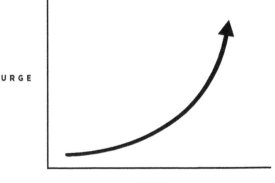

When you actually watch an urge close-up, however, it can surprise you. In reality, an urge is less like a rising line and more like a wave; it swells to a crest or peak, and then if we wait it out it will naturally subside. In other words, urges and cravings—no matter how strong—will eventually go away. This is always the case. Not sometimes— always. Sometimes the urge can take longer to pass and it may feel like it won't ever go away, but trust us, it will pass. Some people call this "urge surfing."

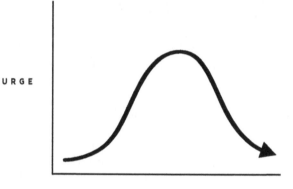

While it takes absolutely zero energy and effort to give in to an urge, choosing to stand, face, and watch an urge takes something else. It takes courage.

Doing this can definitely be challenging, mostly because you want to do something more than just watch it on the recliner with a bag of popcorn. Like having a bug bite itch, you're going to want to do something to make it go away or scratch it, which would only make it worse.

When urge surfing is done right, you do neither of those things. Instead, you stay present, step back from the urge, and watch it—even if it gets tough, even if you have to hang on during moments of intensity. To get to the end of an urge, try focusing on your breathing for a couple of seconds before returning to observe the urge.

You're probably thinking, "Are you kidding? If I don't do something, the urge will win."

Most people think the same thing when they first hear us tell them to try to step back from an urge and observe it. You can see why this is a master-level technique. It's difficult, but it's incredibly powerful and will prove to be one of the most effective ways of responding. Once you become an expert, you'll notice you have the ability to handle impulses in many different situations. It'll take time, but as you start practicing a little bit here and there, you'll be a black belt before you know it.

To recap, we've now explored two different ways to respond with S.T.A.R. The first way deals with replacing the urge by getting engaged with one of your passions. The second way involves stepping back from the urge, so it is separate from who you are, and then simply watching and observing it. As you do this, pay attention to your surroundings and how you feel at that moment, as well as to your body and your thoughts. Then you can simply watch the urge take on a life, grow to full strength, and eventually dissolve into nothing, just like an ocean wave. Ready to try this out?

Imagine you're checking your email and you see an advertisement for pornography in your spam folder. You can feel the desire to open it creeping in. In the past, you would have just given in immediately. However, now that you have S.T.A.R., you decide to step back from the situation, take a few conscious breaths, ask yourself what you really want, and then respond. But this time you respond differently. Instead of replacing the urge with a passion, you decide to stay present and breathe. You stay conscious and recognize the emotions you're feeling. You notice the urge grow to its full strength and just watch it. Like a scientist studying an object's behavior or a hunter in the forest watching an animal, patiently you wait for it to dissipate and scatter. It's hard for a minute, but you stick with it.

Then it's gone. You did it!

"OK, great," you're thinking, "but doesn't the urge or craving just come back again?" Sure, it can and it probably will—especially at first. This will give you plenty of chances to practice. But each time you do, the intensity of the urge will decrease a little bit. And over time, you are slowly retraining your brain to not be driven by any passing urge.

Some days, of course, you may not want to practice S.T.A.R. You may decide to just give in and let the urge win. That's your choice to make, but just realize that each time you do, you're probably setting yourself up for stronger, more powerful urges to come. Did you know that although acting on an impulse relieves the urge in the moment, it actually makes the urge stronger over time because it is reinforcing the brain's neural pathways that lead to using? By contrast, each time you practice S.T.A.R., you are blazing another pathway in your brain. This new pathway says: "There's the urge. I'm no slave, and I won't be moved today—not by this."

The longer you practice S.T.A.R., the less intense urges will be because you're not feeding them or ignoring them. Bottom line: the key to not having to face powerful urges the rest of your life is to learn to respond wisely and powerfully now!

In the meantime, remember to be patient with yourself. It may take time to get the hang of it. You may fall and give in to an urge. It's important that you don't give up. Keep practicing S.T.A.R. until it becomes second nature for you. After a while you'll get the hang of it, and it'll get easier and easier.

The exciting news is that you are learning smart ways to let impulses pass, and building confidence in your ability to endure discomfort and stay present through intensity. We've just spent some significant time exploring different ways to strengthen your mind's capacity to respond to addictive patterns. Take as long as you need to make sure you understand how to implement S.T.A.R. in your life so that you can be prepared when an urge comes.

> **QUICK QUESTION:**
> How do you feel about responding to an urge by stepping back and simply observing the urge grow and eventually dissolve into nothing? Can you see how you may be able to implement that when an urge comes?

 ACTION

What we invite you to do today is practice watching an urge that comes—even if it's just a simple urge to eat some junk food. Rather than just giving in to the urge, notice it arise and how it feels in your body. Practice what we've talked about by watching it and finding the breath in your body as a way to ground yourself. After a couple of minutes, do you notice the urge changing? Keep watching it. It will happen. The good news about this way of responding is that you start to learn not to be a slave to whatever urge or craving arises. You can learn to not get pulled into the urge, and gain a new level of freedom based on your new ability to watch your thoughts and feelings go by without getting pulled in.

STRATEGY #2: ZERO TOLERANCE

We just finished talking about ways you can defend yourself when urges come around. Now it's time to explore some other strategies that will help you prevent future battles.

In Greek mythology, the gorgon monster, Medusa, was feared because her dark powers paralyzed and turned to stone anyone who gazed upon her directly. In spite of her reputation, people were so awe-struck by her appearance that they said, "Oh, I'll be all right if I just look at her a little bit."

In a similar way, sometimes we think just a little pornography won't be that big of a deal. Since pornography is transmitted visually, it is easy to think it's just mental stimulation and not nearly as harmful as a physical drug.

And when someone wants to quit after using for a while, it's very easy to think, "Hey, just a little bit here and there, that won't pull me back in."

Those are illusions; let's review the facts—the brain science: even one look at pornography triggers a rush of pleasure chemicals in the brain and releases other chemicals into the bloodstream. Like blood alcohol levels in a drunk driver, this chemical flood throughout the body can distort judgment and overpower a deeper sense of what's best—effectively blinding individuals to their true desires and interests.

Did you know that studies have actually shown that the blinking lights and rapidly changing images on television and computer screens can have an hypnotic effect on viewers? Where we direct our attention is huge. The effects of what we take in visually are particularly powerful. That rush of pleasure chemicals that pornography use provokes can lead to a dependency for those images and eventually addiction. Therefore, the substance of pornography is as physical as anything—as physical as taking that one drink, shooting up one more time, having one more drag, smoking one more cigarette.

Bottom line: where we look is a big deal; even one glance is enough to stimulate the pleasure chemicals and start the hypnotizing process that blinds us to reality, ultimately leaving individuals mesmerized and effectively "turned to stone" by the modern world's version of Medusa.

So don't be fooled by the "just once" philosophy. Look around you at others and at your own experience. Even just once will leave its mark.

If you are serious about finding the deepest sense of stability, you might consider adopting a zero-tolerance mindset on your way to constructing a porn-free lifestyle. What does this mean? It's more than just a halfhearted attempt. It means more than, "OK, I'll set up a filter." Zero tolerance is about committing to a pornography-free future and not stopping until you get there.

By making the commitment to zero tolerance you are moving in the direction of a complete change, rather than just a general improvement.

Remember that some materials that are not technically pornographic can also set you up for urges to use pornography and deprive you of strength to resist. Television programs, pictures, movies, songs, and books that make light of casual sex and glorify the "anything goes" attitude teach a similar message to that of pornography.

As you determine what to include in your life, identify not only what drags you down but also what lifts you up. Recognize that if you go even one inch past the line you vowed not to cross, it will get in the way of your ability to reason and think straight. A two-inch deviation on a railroad track can turn into thousands of miles of difference later on.

Are you feeling overwhelmed with this zero tolerance section? Take some deep breaths. Just close your eyes and breathe for a minute. Don't worry; what's being said here isn't the "cold turkey" approach. Just like we said earlier, we're talking about committing to a pornography-free future and not stopping until you get there. We're not telling you that you should be at the finish line of the marathon right now, but that you should commit to finishing the race and not quit. Committing to a zero-tolerance mindset will help you get there. You have to keep moving your feet, keep taking actions to overcome the addiction, and that includes being conscious of those things that are preventing you from moving forward—from winning.

That includes being more sensitive to the media around you, since there is a lot of it that will prevent you from moving forward. Ingesting media that glorifies or makes light of sexual things is like trying to run a marathon with weights strapped to your legs. It's going to wear you down and make the effort to cross the finish line much harder—maybe impossible. OK. Breathe again. You cool?

While this doesn't all sound related to pornography, making positive smaller decisions will break you out of the addiction cycle and assist in the commitment to change. Stumbling back into pornography cannot happen without your cooperation on some level.

It should be empowering to know that you have the control. It's up to you. We promise that this fight with addiction will be a lot easier if you commit to a zero-tolerance mindset.

BATTLE STRATEGY #3:

How are you going to implement a zero-tolerance mindset in your life? What boundaries are you going to set for yourself?

(Go to your Battle Strategy in the back of the book on page 229 to answer.)

STRATEGY #3: SECURE YOUR HOME BASE

For anyone facing addiction, it's easy to feel messed up internally. We can be so focused on internal stuff that we sometimes forget just how much our environment can influence us. In any battle, however, ignoring our surroundings can be dangerous.

Some of you know the computer game Sim City. In this game, you as the player are king. Your objective is to create a culture and city that achieves your goals: you decide the manufacturing, the patterns of consumption, the trade, the entertainment, etc.

Imagine, for a moment, the game's manufacturer took a turn to the dark side and came out with a new version entitled *Sim City: Life-Long Addict Edition*, where the goal is to create a society and culture that fosters various kinds of addictions. After passing levels 1 and 2—drugs and tobacco—you're on to the real challenge: creating a society that incubates pornography addiction. What would that look like?

Think about it for a minute. Based on what we see in real life, some good strategies could include:

- Limit the amount of time people spend interacting—the more time alone, the better.
- When they do spend time with people, focus their interaction on superficial things, such as how someone else looks or doesn't look—avoid getting deep and thoughtful at all costs.
- Little or no exercise! And limited sunlight—whatever it takes for their bodies to constantly feel slightly unwell and anxious.
- Make sure individuals are exposed to near-constant media (music, video, phone) with almost no time to sit and contemplate.

Do these conditions sound familiar at all?

The current society we're embedded in is setting us up to fall into serious addictive patterns on a number of levels, and not just with pornography.

It's important that we be aware of this so we can fortify ourselves against the problem. Maybe you really aren't so weak; maybe you're really living in a tough society; and maybe this makes you feel helpless because it's difficult to see how we can change the world around us.

How about we start with something we can control: the environment we embrace immediately around us, specifically in our own home.

Is it possible to create an environment that neutralizes and even combats these larger trends?

On your march toward greater freedom, attention to your home base will be crucial. In every war, you need places of safety where you can be protected and rejuvenated.

What happens when these places have become compromised and infiltrated by the very thing we are battling? It is not uncommon for someone in your situation to be living in a home environment that makes it easy to find the very thing you're trying to escape.

Imagine how difficult it is to quit smoking if the addict is constantly around other smokers. Being frequently reminded of the immediately satisfying effects of something we are trying to quit makes it far more difficult to resist. We are human, and sometimes we feel like we can only take a certain amount of temptation before we cave in. That is why it's crucial to secure your home base—so that it is a source of strength instead of a place of danger and vulnerability. This is another sense of the word fortify: to strengthen and secure a place with reinforcements. When a fortress has a point of weakness—a place where it's too easy to attack—new walls are built.

For those *Fighters* serious about victory, creating a sanctuary is essential for a successful recovery. By placing your fortress on a hill, gravity will be your comrade as your opponent stumbles up the slope, exhausted before he can reach you.

So let's talk about your own home base. Has it been infiltrated by pornography so far? If so, how?

Make a list of ways that pornography is accessible in your home and the different channels through which it has entered in the past, whether that's cable TV, DVDs, tablets, cell phones, gaming devices, home computers, laptops, books, and/or magazines. By listing them out, you'll have a better sense of what areas of your home need the most fortification.

Let's start with TV and movies.

Whether it's HBO or standard cable, you can find a lot of

programming that can lead you to using pornography. It doesn't have to be hard-core pornography to trigger the release of chemicals to your brain. All it takes is a few seconds of arousing content to set you on the path down into the addiction cycle.

Think back to moments after watching television or watching a certain type of movie when you felt most vulnerable. Can you start to notice specific things you saw that made you start to entertain the idea of using?

What about the Internet—porn's favorite playground? This is most likely where the majority of us fall, right? Getting us to stumble across pornography online is where the porn industry focuses most of its energy. And it's pretty darn good at it, isn't it?

Whether it's an endless series of pop-up windows, email spam, relentless advertisements, stealth sites (porn sites with seemingly harmless URLs), or chat rooms, the porn industry knows what it's doing in its efforts to get you hooked.

So rather than fall victim to these cunning attempts, we suggest you draw a kind of firewall between you and pornography. If there is a certain news page or Web site that almost always is a precursor to your using, add it to the filter. Make some hard choices—ESPN instead of Sports Illustrated, NBC instead of HBO. Maybe for you it's not visiting YouTube for the time being. One person we know wanted to stop her habit of sexualized chatting, so she removed the chatting software from her computer and blocked the sites.

If you have a vulnerability to pornography and you spend lots of time wandering the web, before you know it, you're going to get exposed to pornographic material. So what can you do instead? How about this: when you go online, have a mental list of goals or errands to accomplish and a certain time frame for each. We call this browsing with a purpose.

Maybe the list is:
- Check Facebook (of course)
- Check your email
- Write a school paper
- Check out your favorite band's new music video
- And blog about your cat's new sweater vest

Stick to the list, then log off. The second you veer off course, you're setting yourself up for a setback. Apply the zero-tolerance mindset and stick to that list!

Sometimes it requires actually installing software that will filter the Internet and keep your computer safe from inappropriate content. True filtering is difficult to achieve without assistance from someone else in the home to whom you can be accountable. You might have to work with others on keeping the filters bulletproof. It will be best if you can get help from someone who lives with you in doing this, if you feel comfortable. If not, you can at least secure your own room.

If that alone is not doing the trick, a foolproof tactic would be to disconnect from any media sources that provide a temptation and get rid of the Internet for the time being. We know it's kind of hard to believe, but people have been known to survive without it.

During this media detox, only allow yourself to access the Web if necessary and in public areas, such as the city library or a school computer lab.

Realize that the issue of securing your home base is more than an issue of technology. We need to also surround ourselves with pictures, music, and literature that will inspire positive, uplifting thoughts. You have a choice in how safe you want your home environment to be. It would be easy to make a half-hearted effort. We challenge you to be brutally honest with yourself about your home turf vulnerabilities.

Think of this as similar to having a broken door at home, knowing that not only does someone want to attack you, but also that it has happened before—over and over. How committed are you to fixing that door and installing deadbolts?

We may have to be bold in our efforts and rally whatever resources are needed to keep pornography from infiltrating our home if we really want to have a safe haven. Are you willing? How about smaller things? Are you willing to put a filter on your computer? What about moving the computer to another, more public part of the home? Are you willing to get rid of songs or videos, take down pictures, or throw out movies?

You can do it! And remember: for Fighters serious about victory, securing your home base is not a luxury, it's crucial—and possibly the difference between freedom and captivity.

BATTLE STRATEGY #4:

What are you going to do to secure your home base? What are you going to surround yourself with? What are you going to get rid of? What are you going to allow into your life?

(Go to your Battle Strategy in the back of the book on page 229 to answer.)

STRATEGY #4: ANCHORS ("I LOVE YOU MORE")

If an addiction goes on long enough, pornography begins to infiltrate and compromise even our own heart—our core center place. It's now time to start talking about something even bigger than addiction. Think back to the last moment when you used. What was happening— really happening—then? For many of us, in that moment we decided that the only thing that mattered was feeling good *right then* and there. Everything else—previous commitments, other people, other needs—were temporarily ignored. The one thing we cared about more than anything else was how we felt right then.

In a way, even if you hate this addiction, on some level the pornography reflects something you wanted and chose in that moment. In those moments where you use, you want pornography's rush more than anything else.

You see, pornography addiction is far more than just a behavior to stop; it goes way beyond that. The problem is that pornography hijacks our desires and the very things that motivate us.

And because of this, ultimately, your desire to change must be more powerful than your desire for pornography. Let us say that one more time: your desire to change

must be more powerful than your desire for pornography.

It might take a while before that desire for freedom is strong enough on a consistent basis to overcome this addiction. In the meantime, you will need an anchor, something to hold you steady through a raging storm. Is there something—anything—that holds your loyalty stronger than porn?

One guy we know struggled with pornography addiction for years. In his moment of greatest desperation and desire to change, he shattered his computer monitor with a sledgehammer. In a box with the broken pieces of his computer, he left a note for his wife simply stating, "I love you more."

We're not asking you to sledgehammer your computer. We're simply asking you this: Is there anything you love more? Is there something or someone in your life you love more than those videos, those images, and those messages? What or who is it?

It is possible to become so fixed and set on getting away from pornography that we forget or ignore the very things and people in our life that we love more. What if we decide we're not going to ignore them anymore? What if they became anchors for us in this fight?

Most anchors fall into one of three different categories: people, passions, or purpose. Let's talk about people first. This refers to those in your life that you feel are threatened by your addiction, such as a girlfriend/boyfriend, a close friend, your family, or even your future family. The guy who smashed in his computer realized that his wife was more important to him than his pornography addiction, and therefore his wife was an anchor for him.

We talked about passions when we taught you about S.T.A.R. These are activities or ideas that make us tick— things that we truly love doing or pursuing. The more we work on our passions, the happier we become. As many of you know, addictions have a funny way of getting in the way of our true passions. That is why passions can act as an anchor for us; they can counteract the power of an urge when we're not willing to give up doing or working on something we love to satisfy our pornography addiction.

Purpose is something we all strive to find in our lives. Without it, we feel lost and the slightest breeze can sway us off course. Some find purpose in the idea that they want to be a good spouse and parent one day. Others want to be a good example to their peers. Many find purpose in their religious beliefs. Whatever your purpose is, know this: addiction is the enemy to true purpose. They cannot co-exist. Identifying your purpose—or desired purpose— can serve as an anchor for you when you compare the temporary gratification you get when using porn to what you feel deep down is your true purpose in life.

We recommend that you find at least one anchor in each of these categories—people, passions, and purpose—and write them down. This will serve as a reminder to you when things get tough.

So if you want to purge pornography from your life, what will take its place? In the moments when you're bored or lonely or tired or frustrated or anxious, where will you turn besides pornography? If we can't answer these kinds of questions, it's going to be that much harder to really become free. When it gets difficult, remember: this is a real war. And the place where the true battle is happening is your own heart and mind.

Once again, it's not enough to just reject pornography; you need something to hold on to, something or some-one to anchor you. It's time to take command of your own heart and reassert your deeper desires. It's time to practice loving something or someone else more than pornography.

BATTLE STRATEGY #5:

*Write about the things in your life that you love or
desire more than pornography. Try to think of at least
one anchor for each category (people, passions, and
purpose). Explain why each thing is more important
than your addiction to pornography.*

(Go to your Battle Strategy in the back of the book on
page 230 to answer.)

⭐ ACTION

Because our true, deeper desires can sometimes be easy to forget, it can be helpful to create a visual reminder of what those
desires are. Find a small piece of paper that you can carry with
you everywhere you go and write down the anchors you identified for Battle Strategy #5. This can include a picture of your
current family or images of the family you dream of having. If you
don't want to carry it with you everywhere you go, put it up on
your wall.

STRATEGY #5: RELATIONSHIP REALITIES FOR NON-SUPERHEROES

Along the road to recovery, it can be easy to think, "I can
do this. I'm strong enough. I just need to try hard enough,
work harder, and make it happen. I don't need any help."

We all like to believe that kind of thing. But what if it's not always true? What if, at times like this, we're not strong enough on our own? What if just trying harder and working harder is not guaranteed to lead you to freedom? Unless you're secretly a superhero with superhuman powers, you might not be able to overcome this without someone else's help.

We're not talking about therapists, although therapy is great if it's something you have available. We're also not just talking about us at Fight the New Drug, although you've heard plenty about how we're fighting this together. We're actually talking about the people in your life that are around you every day, in close quarters, seeing you and sharing the air you breathe. Among that network of people are a few that may be key to finding your freedom. How? The answer is one huge factor: accountability.

While positive relationships provide a lot of things we all need, when it comes to recovery, one of the most important things good relationships afford us is someone to whom we can be held accountable. Let's illustrate this point with a story someone shared with us.

After years of struggling with addiction, a young man told his father about how he could not quit using pornography after months and months of trying. Despite his efforts to beat pornography, he had repeatedly fallen back into it—and he was scared. Immediately after telling his father, a feeling of relief came to this young man. There was almost an immediate burst of hope as his father listened carefully and cried with him.

After that, everything changed for him, though not overnight. It wasn't just the filtering system that his father helped him set up or the hugs and support he would always get at the end of the check-in conversations. It was also the agreement they reached to talk once a week about how he was doing with his problem. Knowing that his dad would be asking and that he would be sharing with complete honesty added a whole new level of motivation. Trust and hope propelled him gradually to full freedom.

Let us ask you again—this time directly: do you have someone like this in your life? Someone who can stick with you and be willing to ask you tough questions about how you're doing?

While it would be nice to have a parent be this person, someone in your immediate family may not always be the most available or supportive. Having the right person to support you is critical. We'll leave it up to you to decide who you should talk to. We know you'll pick the right person. With that being said, anyone you trust can work: your aunt, uncle, cousin, neighbor, school counselor, friend, or a religious leader. You might find it beneficial to have several people to whom you can be accountable.

As you probably already know, it's easy to keep a pornography problem a secret and not tell anyone. Just as accountability can help you break free, isolation can make the problem worse. But the good news is your participation in this program may be a sign that you're willing to break out of isolation on the issue.

Look, we understand how difficult it can be to share this problem with someone else. It's normal to feel embarrassed or shameful. The problem is, if you don't reach out now, it will likely be a lot harder later on, because the deeper your addiction gets the more motivation you'll have to hide it and keep it secret. Realize that many people have struggled with this problem, and you are not alone.

So think twice about doing this on your own. If you do happen to think you've got some superhuman powers, remember—even superheroes rely on a sidekick in their hour of need.

BATTLE STRATEGY #6:

Write out a list of individuals that you could imagine
being supportive of your desire to recover. This could
include any family members, religious leaders, and oth-
er people you trust. Keep this list around as you think
about having accountability partners.

(Go to your Battle Strategy in the back of the book on
page 230 to answer.)

STRATEGY #6: BATTLE TRACKER

In the fight that we're exploring together, it's easy to focus
on the times we fail and fall—coming away with a vision
centered around only our bad times. What about the days
we are strong? The times we let the urge pass?

You may not have thought to keep track of good days—or
of any days for that matter. Most people rarely keep track
of good or bad days, and therefore they don't have a clear
picture of what kind of addiction they're really dealing
with. How often do you give in to your addiction? What
is the longest you've been able to go without a setback?
What time of day do you normally struggle the most?
What kinds of activities lead you to using most often?

These are the types of questions that addicts who are serious about recovery often consider. They know exactly
when their last several setbacks were and how much time
there was between each setback. They can also start to see
patterns emerge, such as the time of day or which day of
the week they struggle the most. That is why if you ask
a former alcoholic how long it's been since they had their
last sip of alcohol, they can often tell you down to the very

hour. They know that date as well as they know their own birthday. One recovering alcoholic told us that he doesn't focus on getting to five years from now. Instead, he focuses on conquering each day and sometimes each hour. At first that was what it took, he told us; but now that he has been sober for more than five years, he says that it has become much easier and that he didn't know he could be so happy.

You see, recovering addicts track that information to keep them strong even when they feel vulnerable. Knowing that data about your own addiction is crucial, because it will not only help you see patterns in your addiction, but it will also give you motivation as you measure your successes.

To help you start tracking, we are going to give you a very simple way to measure this information. At the back of this book you will see what we call a Battle Tracker (found on page 228), which is essentially a calendar to track your battles and your victories. You'll notice that each day has three separate columns that represent morning, afternoon, and night. In each column there are four different boxes with a numerical value ranging from 0 to 3. Each number represents the intensity of a particular urge—or what we like to call a battle.

For example, if a strong urge to view pornography hits you in the morning, then you would put an X in the very top box of the morning column. If you had no urge to view pornography in the afternoon, then you would put an X at the very bottom box in the afternoon column indicating that you had no battles during that time of day. Giving each battle a rating is important. At first, you may stumble with a level 1 battle, but as you get stronger you may get to the point where you experience two separate level 3 battles in a single day without having a setback. Each victory will make you stronger for the next battle.

You'll also notice a place to mark whether or not you had a setback that day. It's never easy to admit temporary defeat, but when it does happen it is important that you acknowledge it. Some of our Fighters mark this box with a red X. The fewer X's they see in a given month, the better. During your first few months you may experience several more defeats than you had hoped. However, those who stick to it and keep using their Battle Tracker can see their progress over time.

There's also space on your Battle Tracker to specify where the setback occurred and what triggered that particular battle (TV, browsing the web, a billboard, etc.). This will help you recognize patterns and give you the necessary information to make adjustments and gain an advantage over your addiction.

One of our Fighters described the Battle Tracker as being one of his most powerful weapons. When you can actually see and record your day-to-day battles and track your successes and setbacks, you can gain an understanding that will give clarity and strength to your fight against pornography.

In addition to measuring your behaviors, you might also consider setting short-term goals. Short-term goals can make a larger goal—like overcoming your addiction— seem manageable. These goals could focus on slightly adjusting your schedule to avoid moments of possible vulnerability. For example, if you've found that late nights are often when you give in to urges, you might set a goal to go to bed earlier to avoid staying up too late. Your goals could also focus on breaking your longest streak with no setbacks, or setting up a weekly sit-down with your accountability partner to go over your progress. Tracking your daily progress with the Battle Tracker will also help you recognize which goals were most effective in helping you win battles.

Make sure when you set short- or long-term goals that they follow the S.M.A.R.T. goals formula. This stands for goals that are Specific, Measurable, Achievable, Realistic, and Time-Bound.

Let's test a couple of goals out and see if they pass as S.M.A.R.T. goals test.

Goal #1: Be better.

Is it specific? Not really. What are we supposed to be better at? Is it measurable? Um, nope. Is it achievable? Well, yeah but according to what? Is it realistic? Sure, we can always be better, but again, it's a little too vague. Is it time-bound? Not at all.

Goal #2: This month I am only going to get on the Internet on my home computer (which is located in the family room) and will only use it between 3 p.m. to 6 p.m. each day.

Is it specific? Very. Is it measurable? Yep, we can measure exactly what days we did and did not accomplish this goal. Is it achievable? You bet. Is it realistic? Absolutely. Is it time-bound? Once again, yes. We clearly stated that this was a daily goal that will last the duration of the entire month.

By following this formula you will be able to set effective and powerful goals. From this point on we encourage you to start using your Battle Tracker and to set short-term goals. Combine this offensive strategy with the strategies discussed earlier and you'll really start to become a warrior—a real Fighter!

CHECK-IN

Congratulations on completing Basic Training. But don't think that just because you finished reading this chapter means that you can stop practicing what you've learned. Not even close. We'll say it again: this is going to take practice— and a lot of it. You will need to practice and develop your strategies in order to be serious about recovery. How serious you are about daily practice could make the difference between how free you are three months, six months, or twelve months from now.

That being said, let's do a quick practice with S.T.A.R. together right now. You ready? OK, here we go.

Of course, you're probably not dealing with an urge to look at pornography at this very moment, but that doesn't stop us from being able to practice the process of using S.T.A.R. so that we are prepared when an urge does hit.

First, let us ask you how it has been going for you. How many times have you had a chance to use S.T.A.R. in your daily battles? Of those times when you used S.T.A.R., what was your experience like? How, if at all, did it impact your decisions? It's OK to still be figuring it out. It may take some time to make S.T.A.R. a natural part of the process.

Right now we want you to step back—this time,

not from an urge but from your current situation. Slow down and observe your surroundings. Detach yourself from the room you're in, the book in your hand, and the people around. Focus your visual attention on a single spot or close your eyes to remove distractions. Can you feel your life slowing down just a bit? Now, take a few conscious breaths. Notice the air slowly filling your lungs and then release. Keep slowly breathing in and out. As time seems to slow down, can you start to feel a sense of control and clarity?

Do you think you're in a good place to ask yourself what you really want? You should be in a calm state to think clearly and really be in tune with what is important to you in the short- and long-term.

At this point, you should be ready to respond. Do you feel comfortable making a decision and moving forward in a direction that makes sense?

Wouldn't it be great if you could be this in-control when an urge to view pornography hit you? You can be! That is the whole point of S.T.A.R. As you keep practicing and get better at each of the four steps, you can gain a control that will allow you to make the choices you really want— not what your addiction wants.

Try practicing S.T.A.R. several times a day— with or without an urge present.

CHAPTER FOUR ⟫⟫ FORTIFY YOURSELF

BUILDING THE LIFE YOU REALLY WANT

You just finished Basic Training and you now have some defensive skills you can pull out whenever you need them—as well as some strategies to start going on the offensive against this addiction. Although these will all take some practice to get down, that's no problem. You're not scared by a little bit of work, right?

If these skills and strategies were the only thing you took away and the program ended now, we'd be excited at what you could do in the months ahead. As you get stronger and stronger, you will become more and more successful in avoiding the traps that used to ensnare you.

"OK," you're probably thinking, "that's great—help to win more battles. I do want that. But what about the rest of my life ahead? Am I going to be fighting these same battles forever?"

Some people say that this will always be a battle for you— that you'll always struggle with this. Don't believe that! We don't! With a smart, focused effort, you can get to a place where you no longer struggle and eventually feel completely free from your addiction.

Remember what we said earlier about brain plasticity? We weren't joking. If the actual physiological patterns in our brain can change, what does that mean about other patterns in our behavior, thoughts, and even our desires? You got it: they can also change and evolve over time. Although you may still have more vulnerability to pornography than someone else, over time the weight of addiction can eventually get lighter and lighter to the point where you don't even feel its presence in your life.

If you're serious about pursuing this kind of a deeper level of change and freedom, then it's time to take this to the next level of the fight. What exactly do we mean?

Rather than hacking at the branches of your addiction, what if we decided to dive deeper, getting at the roots of your challenge in a way that would help you move out of this trap for good? Think about the last time you were in a dark room. If you wanted that to change, what did you do? Did you try turning off the darkness? No, of course not.

Obviously, it makes no sense to attempt to make physical darkness go away by shutting it off—and yet we often assume this will work with emotional and mental darkness. Rather than trying to "turn off" the darkness in a room, the answer is turning on a light. In the laws of the universe, light governs darkness—once light comes, darkness has to leave. You see, darkness cannot exist where light is. In fact, darkness by definition is the absence of light.

Simply put, if we want to really get away from pornography, we can't focus all our energies on battling the "darkness" itself. We have to focus some energy on not only turning away, but also on turning toward something else. What if you started filling up your life with other things—activities and habits that begin to fulfill you and start to form the life you always wanted to live? Could moving this direction actually mean the addiction eventually has to leave—each step strangling and choking its power?

Rather than only finding more ways to resist the addiction or fight the darkness, it's time to talk about filling up your life with light by creating healthy habits that make life so fulfilling that pornography will become a nuisance.

In summary, you've naturally been focusing a lot on what not to do, which is understandable and important. However, we're talking about shifting the main focus to a different place: what to do.

So, what should you do? What kinds of things and activities are we talking about? To help you explore these possibilities we decided to look at the research and find anything that may be setting you up to be vulnerable to addiction.

It's important to know that while you will sometimes hear talk of "the cause" of an addiction, there is no single cause of pornography addiction—no one thing responsible for it all. There are many things that can set us up for addiction. Scientists call these contributors "risk factors" or "vulnerabilities."

Based on risk factor studies, we've identified several different areas that deserve some attention. Because there are lots of them, we've summarized them in a survey for you. In the next section you will be able to take the Fortify Yourself Inventory, which will help you recognize areas of vulnerability and strength in your life. In later chapters you will have a chance to look at additional areas of your life and pinpoint possible vulnerabilities.

FORTIFY YOUR LIFE

FORTIFY YOUR LIFE INVENTORY

Instructions: The following inventory is a way of helping you explore the potential contributors to addiction. Each question comes from a research study that correlates or connects this issue to online addiction of some kind. There is no single cause of addiction. Instead, the focus here is the "root system" that underlies addiction—exploring both areas of vulnerability and areas of strength.

To score your inventory, count the number of times you answered "yes" in each section and compare that total number to the scoring metric at the bottom of each section to find out whether or not that area would be considered a vulnerability or a strength in your life.

PAST CHALLENGES		
1. Have you ever had any brain damage, such as from an accident?	Y	N
2. Were you ever physically abused in your past in any way?	Y	N
3. Were you ever sexually abused in your past in any way?	Y	N
4. If you have experienced abuse of any kind, have you kept it to yourself?	Y	N
5. Have you ever observed abuse or violence from a parent figure to other children in your family?	Y	N
6. Have you ever observed abuse or violence between your parents or guardians?	Y	N

*If you answered "yes" to one or more questions, this section would be considered a vulnerability. If you answered "no" to all six question, this section would be considered a strength.

OVERALL CONTROL IN YOUR LIFE

1. Do you often make impulsive decisions (without much thought)? Y N
2. Are you sexually active (with another person)? Y N
3. Do you have any other behaviors that you have a hard time stopping? Y N
4. Do you smoke nicotine or marijuana? Y N
5. Do you drink alcohol? Y N
6. Do you take illegal drugs of any kind? Y N
7. Do you gamble online and have a hard time stopping? Y N
8. Do you shop excessively and have a hard time stopping? Y N
9. Do you exercise so much that people worry you're overdoing it? Y N
10. Independent of pornography, do you often feel that you have to be on the Internet most of the time? Y N
11. To your knowledge, are there others in your family (siblings, parents) who view pornography? Y N
12. Do you have family members that struggle with other addictions, such as to alcohol, cigarettes, or drugs? Y N

*If you answered "yes" to two or more questions, this section would be considered a vulnerability.
If you answered "no" to 11 or more questions, this section would be considered a strength.

OVERALL HEALTH

1. Do you regularly struggle with sleep such as having a hard time getting to sleep, not getting a good night's sleep, sleeping too long, or other sleep problems? Y N
2. Are you often sleepy during the day? Y N
3. Do you find yourself avoiding opportunities to exercise? Y N
4. Do you find yourself eating more processed foods rather than whole foods (vegetables, fruit, or whole grains)? Y N
5. Do you drink large amounts of coffee, energy drinks, or other caffeinated beverages? Y N
6. Do you eat lots of candy, desserts, or other treats? Y N
7. Is it pretty common that you skip breakfast? Y N

*If you answered "yes" to two or more questions, this section would be considered a vulnerability.
If you answered "no" to six or more questions, this section would be considered a strength.

MEANING AND PURPOSE

	Y	N
1. Would you say you are unsatisfied with your daily life?	☐	☐
2. Do you find yourself believing that there is little to no purpose to life?	☐	☐
3. Would you say that religion or faith is not important to you?	☐	☐
4. Do you sometimes wish you could escape your life?	☐	☐
5. Do you feel a lot of guilt about choices you've made in the past?	☐	☐
6. Are you pretty hard on yourself usually (e.g., blaming, self-condemning)?	☐	☐
7. Do you often feel worthless as a person?	☐	☐
8. Do you often feel depressed or hopeless?	☐	☐
9. Have you lost interest or pleasure in activities you used to enjoy?	☐	☐
10. Do you often feel anxious or fearful?	☐	☐
11. Do you sometimes obsess so much about something that you have a hard time not thinking about it?	☐	☐
12. Are you dissatisfied with your body, looks, or weight?	☐	☐
13. Do you sometimes feel detached from your body and the surrounding world?	☐	☐

*If you answered "yes" to two or more questions, this section would be considered a vulnerability.
 If you answered "no" to 12 or more questions, this section would be considered a strength.

FACING HARD THINGS IN THE PAST

One thing that can set people up for any kind of addiction is a difficult past experience, especially if it hasn't yet been resolved. There are lots of different challenges that can come up in your life, such as losing a family member or friend, or abuse. Let's take a moment and focus on abuse—of any kind.

We used to think abuse was rare and only happened to a small segment of the population, but society knows better now. We now know that several forms of abuse are far too common—especially to children. Sometimes abuse comes from a neighbor or a stranger. Other times it comes from someone right in your own family—from people who are supposed to be there to protect and care for you.

It can be hard to understand why someone who is supposed to love you would hit you, slap you, or physically hurt you in any way. That is called physical abuse, and it's not right. It's also difficult to understand why someone who is supposed to love you would call you names and say other things that make you feel worthless. That's called emotional abuse, and that's also very wrong. Both of these types of abuse can lead an individual toward addictive behaviors. This happens in most cases because the person who was abused often looks for an escape from a hard reality that they don't know how to deal with appropriately.

However, there is another type of abuse that also deserves a discussion. Can you guess what it is? We'll give you a hint: it has been closely linked to pornography addiction. That's right, sexual abuse.

It's hard to understand why an adult would do something sexual to a child. There is also no excuse for that—none. What you may not know is that there is a significant link between abusing children sexually and pornography use.

Isn't that interesting? An individual's insatiable appetite for pornography can lead that person to act out their fantasies on those around them. Children are often targeted because they are young and can be controlled. Not only are there links between sexual child abuse and pornography use among abusers, but there is also a predisposition to use pornography among the abused.

Did you catch that? It's important so we'll say it again. Many people who were abused as children grow up struggling with their sexuality and often turn to pornography to escape hard realities.

If abuse of any kind has happened in your past, you need to know something right now: no matter what you think, it's not your fault. You did not deserve to be treated that way. No one does. And you don't have to let those past challenges continue to mess with your life.

There is another kind of abuse that many don't recognize. It is witnessing others get abused, such as another sibling or one of your parents. Witnessing abuse to a parent or sibling can be extremely painful and traumatizing. If you have experienced or witnessed any of these—physical abuse, emotional abuse, or sexual abuse—it's almost certainly one of the things making it harder for you to turn away from pornography.

Because experiences of abuse are so traumatic and painful, they often lead to many other problems, ranging from depression to anxiety and even to eating disorders. This happens because our brains and bodies were designed to be loved and protected, not attacked. When trauma occurs, the healthiest thing to do is to recognize what happened and that it was wrong; try to understand why it took place; and move forward. But this isn't what usually happens. Instead, we often ignore painful experiences, suppress them, and pretend they didn't happen. We try to avoid talking or thinking about what happened, hoping that maybe the effects will just go away. This kind of pain usually doesn't just go away on its own, though; it still bothers us somewhere in our subconscious. It weighs us down. We still hurt from it, so we look for some way to hurt less, ways to feel better. Pornography can become a distraction from the pain—our drug of choice.

Fortunately, there are many healthy ways to get rid of this weight. One way is to lean on someone else. It takes courage to really share with and confide in someone else, even when it's with someone you trust. You may wonder, "What's the point in talking about this if we can't go back in time and change anything? Wouldn't people be better off just forgetting about it?"

While it's true that it can be unhealthy to dissect everything about a painful experience, it's also true that the past can continue to negatively influence us if we don't face it in a healthy way. Like secrecy with addiction, secrecy about past abuse can strengthen that abuse's hold over us. Breaking that secrecy can allow us to start healing at the deepest level.

We're not talking about doing anything dramatic. In fact, what we're suggesting is that you just talk about any past abuse with someone you trust and love—and who you know loves you. Set aside a time with that person, explaining ahead of time that you need privacy and a time when they can give you their full attention, and then share with them what happened to you.

Then take a breath and talk to them. Although it can be hard to open up about such a difficult topic, trust us: you will feel relief in doing so, and not just over the short-term. Talking out hard experiences can help you know how to process them and learn what you need to do to let them pass, so that you don't have to keep carrying the pain they caused forever.

If it makes you more comfortable, you can talk with some-one who has professional training, such as a school coun-selor or therapist. These kinds of professionals can help you talk about and process the experience.

What if you're not ready? That's OK. When you are ready, you'll know. Just plan on doing it at some point. As you move in this direction, you can even come to the point where you're able to consider something like forgiveness.

"Hold on," you might be thinking. "How could I forgive someone that did such horrible things to me?"

We get it. This isn't an easy thing to consider.

Eventually, in order to move on and stop carrying this burden, forgiveness may need to be a part of your pro-cess, too. One of our favorite quotes is from Paul Boese: "Forgiveness does not change the past, but it does enlarge the future."

Don't make the mistake of thinking that by forgiving someone you would be indicating that what that person did to you was right or OK. That is not true at all. What they did to you was wrong and will never be right. Per-haps the most important thing to remember about for-giveness is that it's not for the person that hurt you; it's for you. Once you sincerely forgive, you'll notice a weight lifted—gone. You'll start to feel empathy for the abuser and you'll see yourself rise to a new sense of freedom. It's worth it. We promise.

BATTLE STRATEGY #7:

If this area is relevant to you and you have not been able to fully process some past experiences, find and talk to a trusted adult. Who, specifically, can you talk to? When do you plan to talk to them?

(Go to your Battle Strategy in the back of the book on page 231 to answer.)

REGAINING CONTROL IN YOUR LIFE

We live in a society that throws many things in our face that seem to demand a response: "Obey your thirst!" in the words of one commercial.

So maybe it's not surprising that many of us end up getting swept away with lots of different habits, some good and others not so good. Do you know anyone that struggles with their weight? How about a 7-hour-a-day TV watcher? Or an 8-hour-a-day gamer? Or someone who won't stop shopping even when their credit line has run out?

You get the picture. Self-control isn't easy in a society serving up 100 quick and immediate ways to feel better NOW. That's pretty much why we're here—to help you gain control in your life. Like we said before, we're not here to give you a quick fix to your problems. We want to give you long-lasting solutions and ways to feel better tomorrow and every day after that.

If you can't direct your own life, then you've given that

control over to someone or something else. And who wants that? Self-control is a crucial part of a healthy, happy life. Those who don't have it end up hurting themselves and those they love immensely. That's because relationships and love require sacrifice.

If you don't have the ability to let go of some of the immediate gratifications in life, then you won't be reliable and constant in a relationship. Rather than being guided by the needs of others, you'll be driven by whatever feeling you're having in a given moment.

In fact, research shows that one area of addictive struggle can feed into another. For instance, if you binge on a ton of doughnuts, in the hours afterward, you're probably going to be more likely to turn to pornography.

Why is this? It's actually pretty simple. These compulsive habits are exercising the same general pathways, sparking the same kind of chemical rush that is seen with pornography. In this way, each time you engage in any addictive habit, you're priming the brain, "greasing the wheels" in a sense, to want more pornography.

As you saw in the Fortify Yourself Inventory, many kinds of addictive habits can set someone up for pornography addiction. Some who struggle with their temper, for instance, by getting angry easily and regularly, are also more likely to have a pornography problem. The same is true with a compulsion to inflict self-harm and cut oneself. If you struggle with any addictive behavior—such as gambling, excessive shopping, alcohol, drugs, anger, self-harm, overeating/binge eating, under-eating, etc.— it's probably feeding into and fueling your pornography problem as well.

When several addictions exist together, it can get especially discouraging. You may hear from others, "You're just an impulsive person," or "Maybe you've got an addictive personality."

Don't believe them. Remember, it's very common for several addictions to exist at once. And even more to the point: this isn't who you are. We've said that before, and we'll say it again, and we'll say it to you personally if you want to call us on the phone!

The good news is that as you take control of one addiction, it will start to loosen the others' grip. Another way of thinking about it is to recognize that if you're struggling with multiple addictions, they are actually the same problem—namely, turning to something as a "fix" to escape from the discomforts of life. That's the definition of any addictive behavior.

So think about your life. What other addictions or compulsive behaviors do you see? Are there ways that you try and escape from the discomforts of life other than through pornography? We bet you've never considered that those other behaviors could be linked to your pornography addiction, have you? But they are!

OK, so now you're thinking: "Now what? How can I get rid of my addictive behaviors?" Wait, didn't we talk about something like that in the last chapter? That's right. In fact, nearly everything that we discussed in Basic Training can help with pretty much any other addiction.

So next time you want to turn to a quick-fix, try using S.T.A.R. or leveraging one of the other strategies against whatever you are facing.

QUICK QUESTION:
What other unhealthy habits have you used or seen others use to escape the discomforts of life?

BATTLE STRATEGY #8:

*After taking a deeper look into the rest of your life,
can you identify any other areas that seem a little out
of control? Write them down and then brainstorm
different ideas to help you kick these other unwanted
behaviors.*

(Go to your Battle Strategy in the back of the book on
page 231 to answer.)

RECHARGING YOUR BODY

Some of the most interesting things that influence any
addiction (including pornography) are basic things such
as sleep, nutrition, and exercise. "OK," you're thinking,
"how do my eating, sleeping, and exercise habits influence my addiction?"

We'll tell you. Across many research studies on lifestyle
factors that affect addictions, some things that comes up
loud and clear are the "big three"—nutrition, exercise,
and sleep. Each of these makes a huge difference in the
quality of our mood and our overall mental and emotional well-being. Both separately and in combination,
they impact anything from depression and anxiety to how
well we can focus our attention at any given moment.

You didn't need any scientist to tell you that, though. Just
think of the last time you binged on Halloween candy or
spent the whole day inside, sitting around. How did you
feel? Sometimes things that can feel good in the moment
can really make us feel not-so-good later on. When we
pay attention, we begin to notice how much these little

patterns of sleep, eating, or exercise impact our mood. When we don't feel well, it's all too easy to scramble, once again, for some way—any way—to feel better.

That's what we explored earlier—that our attempts to avoid the discomforts of life often set us on the path toward using. Whenever the body is unbalanced, it will be more likely to crave anything and everything to try and find relief.

So in addition to all the other things you're doing to get stronger, you can also fortify yourself by improving your basic wellbeing by making some adjustments in your overall physical lifestyle.

Let's take a look at your sleeping habits. A recent study by the National Sleep Foundation found that during the school year, most American teenagers are not getting the sleep they need (National Sleep Foundation, 2011).

Sufficient sleep is especially crucial for anyone wanting to find true recovery from addiction. Why would this matter? It's simple. Your brain and body actually recharge and repair during sleep. When we go without it, our ability to reason and think clearly is impaired. Did you know that studies have actually shown that a sleepy driver is about as dangerous as a drunk driver?

Bottom line: a tired brain and cloudy mind will leave you vulnerable to whatever craving hits you. A lack of sleep can inhibit your judgment, so when that urge to use pornography comes around, you're less prepared to fight it.

Make healthy amounts of sleep a top priority. If anything is getting in the way of getting enough sleep, take it very seriously, because if it's getting in the way of your sleep then it's also getting in the way of your recovery.

In addition to sleep, another way to recharge your body is to check out what kind of fuel you're giving it.

Have you ever tried putting maple syrup or Kool-Aid in the gas tank of a car? We're not asking you to try this at home, but what if you did? How far would you get in that car? It sounds dumb, but let's be honest: we're sometimes just as dumb with our own body by skipping breakfast, tanking down stuff it doesn't need or want, and denying it sleep. How can we expect it to run well? When the body doesn't run well, you're not going to have as much energy and strength to do what you really want. You're going to be more liable to being swept away into the addiction cycle.

So what can be done? Don't worry—we're not talking about cutting out certain kinds of food and becoming a health nut. We're not even talking about telling you what things you should or shouldn't eat.

Rather than listening to anyone else tell you what to eat, why not listen to your own body? We're just talking about paying closer attention to what your body needs and wants.

When our bodies are deprived of any need, whether it's nutrition or sleep, we begin to seek out something to relieve the discomfort—especially replacements that make the body feel immediately satisfied. Being hungry or tired can make anyone vulnerable to a relapse to pornography or any other addiction.

All right, let's finish up this discussion with one more thing. While recharging your body through rest and good fuel is important, if you really want to supercharge it, then try something really powerful: moving around.

Although there is a lot of discussion about physical activity these days, Americans still do a ton of sitting around. What's so wrong with sitting? Nothing, of course, unless you don't do anything else. Without movement and activity of some sort, we are starving our brain in another way and setting it up for the same ol' same ol' patterns.

What about the reverse? What if we bumped up our activity level? In the late 1990s, Dr. Van Praag and his colleagues at the Laboratory of Genetics at the Salk Institute in San Diego, CA, showed that exercise increases neurogenesis—that's when new brain cells are made.

When you exercise, a flood of oxygen heads to your brain and a number of other processes are triggered that help your brain to grow. So by exercising, we're actually rewiring the brain in a healthy way, and giving our brain an extra boost to function at peak performance!

We're not saying you need to become an Olympic gold medalist. We're just talking about moving more.

Rather than trying to change something dramatic, it can be helpful to find ways to slowly increase your level of physical activity. While sometimes a specialized program can be helpful, there are also other ways to increase physical activity in your life. Let's get creative:

- Taking the stairs rather than the elevator
- Not driving or asking for rides everywhere you need to go, so you can walk or bike
- Fully participating in activities during gym class at school

- Trying out hikes or trails in your area
- Spending time at a park
- Getting friends together to play sports
- Doing a few sit-ups or push-ups before jumping in the shower
- If you drive, parking at the back of the parking lot when you head to the mall
- Getting a bike at a yard sale, if you don't have one

Studies are showing that poor health can cause us to be more susceptible to impulsive decisions. Fighting to develop better health habits will indirectly help us fight the larger battle against porn. Let's do it!

BATTLE STRATEGY #9:

How would it feel to commit to being truly physically healthy? No matter where you are with addiction, making this decision would be one step closer to your freedom. What can you do to increase your physical activity? What can you do to improve your eating habits? What time are you going to go to bed and what time are you going to wake up every day?

(Go to your Battle Strategy in the back of the book on page 232 to answer.)

⭐ ACTION

For the next week, try spending an additional 15 minutes a day outside doing something you like. This could be going on a walk, going on a bike ride, playing basketball, taking photos, throwing a Frisbee, playing with your dog, etc.

FINDING MEANING AND PURPOSE

Did you know that low self-esteem can actually make you more vulnerable to addictive behaviors? (Hardoon, Gupta & Deverensky, 2004) Why do you think that is? After you think about it for a second, it's pretty obvious, isn't it?

The worse you feel about yourself, the more you're going to seek out ways to feel accepted, important, and in control. Often times we turn to pornography because it gives us a false sense of connection with those on the computer screen or magazine page. However, by turning to pornography or any other addictive behavior to escape from feelings of worthlessness, we are actually pouring fuel on the fire.

We have a friend that struggled with low self-esteem and pornography addiction who described the cycle the two conditions created this way: "It's funny. Because of my low self-esteem, I found myself turning to pornography for relief, but afterwards I would actually feel worse and my self-esteem would get even lower. So without seeing the connection between the two, I would turn back to the very thing that was making it worse."

His observation is consistent with research that clearly shows the same pattern: turning to addictions such as alcohol, street drugs, or pornography for relief from depression, loneliness, or self-hatred pushes individuals deeper into those same emotional ruts. The deeper we go, the more intensely we look for an escape. Do you see the downward spiral?

So low self-esteem can be made worse through pornography addiction; but get this: did you also know that porn can actually cause low self-esteem?

Due to this pattern, our sense of purpose and self-worth

can take a beating by any addiction. When we're giving our brain a dopamine rush over and over in response to a screen or magazine image, what do you think happens when we get up from our chair and turn back to real life?

That's right: it's boring! Think about it; real life can sometimes seem dull when compared to those videos and images. We can start to feel less and less enthusiastic about anything, and that includes ourselves—our worth and well-being.

People with a pornography addiction simply stop caring that much about their own lives. They report feeling a loss of their sense of hope, purpose, and meaning in life.

And the cycle continues: this low mood then sets us up to think we want and need more of that artificial dopamine rush of pornography. After all, when any of us feels low and terrible, we're going to want relief.

And when we try to escape those bad feelings through pornography or other harmful substances, we're launching into the addiction cycle we discussed earlier. Is there another way to handle this emotional pain?

What if we thought about a low mood or a feeling of hopelessness like an alarm system going off in the body? When your finger touches a hot stove, the pain you feel hurts—but it's also telling you something, right? It's telling you to take your finger off the hot stove! What if your body didn't tell you that you should take your finger off the hot stove? We would have far more serious injuries and probably be missing a few limbs, wouldn't we? It's a good thing we feel pain, because it helps us make adjustments.

Physical and emotional pain are similar. Although they hurt, feelings of being down, sad, anxious, or angry tell us something important about our lives. For one, this emotional pain may be telling you to get away from this habit as fast as you can. As you notice yourself feeling weighed down and in pain, try taking that as motivation for everything you're practicing, learning, and putting into place.

And here's the best news of all: as you practice the strategies you learned in Basic Training, guess what begins to happen—the reverse of the pattern above. Unlike pornography, which erodes your sense of meaning and purpose, being free from porn addiction helps restore those back to your life.

As you begin to taper off of artificial stimulation and acclimate again to healthy levels of emotion, the brain actually starts to remember that real life is pleasurable and worth enjoying.

Notice how different this is from how we usually talk about self-esteem in society. It's common to hear that we just need to love ourselves and realize we're special.

Our approach is different. Instead of trying to finesse feelings by simply saying, "You're great, just tell yourself that," we're talking about going to work building a life you can believe in, a life where you are offering something to the world, where your energies matter, where you are making a difference for someone. As you do so, it will change everything. You'll notice a deep sense of purpose and contribution.

Here are a few activities that can help you build this kind of life:

- Spend time with people that build you up, rather than tear you down
- Take some time to read and contemplate what you really believe
- Set small goals and achieve them
- Recognize your strengths and what you do well

- Help others around you improve their situations
- Get involved with and contribute to a cause greater than yourself
- Look for the good in those around you—everyone around you
- Work hard at turning your interests into skills
- Speak in a British accent (for some reason that always works)

For many who face serious addiction, spirituality—whatever you define that to be—can also play a crucial role in finding freedom. Many find strength in turning to a higher power. If this is something that works for you, use it!

While it's important to break free from your porn addiction, or any addiction for that matter, having light to fill the void in your life that pornography used to fill is what is really going to give you meaning and purpose.

QUICK QUESTION:
Think back to one of the happiest times in your life. Try to analyze why it was a happy time. What were you involved with? Who were your friends? What did you believe in?

BATTLE STRATEGY #10:

Make a list of three things that you can begin to implement into your life that will help build your sense of self-worth.

(Go to your Battle Strategy in the back of the book on page 232 to answer.)

CHECK-IN

You're half way through the *Fortify* program and doing a great job! Are you ready for another check-in?

Let's spend a little more time with S.T.A.R. and focus this check-in on responding. Have you been practicing different ways to respond? Have you tried detaching yourself from the urge and watching it without acting on it? Not easy, is it? Some of you may be getting a handle on it and realizing just how powerful it can be. Others of you may be thinking, "I don't get it. I keep trying and I just can't figure it out."

Regardless of where you're at, this exercise will help you grasp the concept a little better and help you start applying it in battle. You see, the idea of simply watching the urge swell and subside over time without acting on it requires you to strengthen specific mental muscles—muscles you probably didn't even know you had.

It's like being a first time skier: it doesn't matter how many Warren Miller films you've seen; when you're actually on that mountain you're going to have to use muscles you never knew you had in order to turn properly. Talking about what you need to do when an urge hits and actually doing it are not the same thing. We can explain what to do and how it's done until we're blue in the face, but it may never sink in for you. It's not until you put it into practice and actually try it out that you will start to understand its true power.

So let's practice. Rather than giving you a fabricated scenario to imagine, we want you to practice using the actual mental muscles needed to successfully watch an urge and not act on it.

Wherever you are right now, we want you to close your eyes and mentally step back from everything around you. Calmly listen to the sounds around you. Pay attention to your body and how it feels. Recognize your thoughts and emotions. How do you feel in this very moment? What thoughts are popping up in your mind? Whatever they are—good or bad—detach yourself from those thoughts and emotions and watch them without doing anything. Mentally separate them from your body and observe them. Recognize that they have no control over you.

If you feel yourself getting pulled into or controlled by a thought or emotion, quickly focus on your breathing to anchor your mind. Watch your thoughts and emotions take on a life of their own and eventually dissipate.

How'd it go? Did it feel like time slowed down a little? That's a good thing. By slowing down your decision-making process and connecting with your core desires, you are more likely to stay in control during a battle.

Practice this over and over until you get the hang of it. Do it several times a day—urge or no urge. By working these mental muscles you will eventually be strong enough to try the technique out on an actual urge and win!

CHAPTER FIVE  FORTIFY
YOUR RELATIONSHIPS

FORTIFY YOUR RELATIONSHIPS

FORTIFY YOUR RELATIONSHIPS INVENTORY

Instructions: The following inventory is a way of helping you explore the potential contributors to addiction that might be affecting you. Each question comes from a research study that correlates or connects the issue discussed to online addiction of some kind.

Rather than searching for one single cause of addiction, the focus here is the root system that underlies addiction and explores both areas of vulnerability and areas of strength.

To score your inventory, count the number of times you answered "yes" in each section and compare that total number to the scoring metric at the bottom of each section to find out whether that area would be considered a vulnerability or a strength in your life.

CONNECTION AND COMMUNITY

1. Are you unhappy with your current family relationships? ☐Y ☐N
2. Do you usually not feel the support of family and friends? ☐Y ☐N
3. Does your family feel disconnected and distant as a whole? ☐Y ☐N
4. Would you describe your family's communication style as unhealthy? ☐Y ☐N
5. Have you received little or limited nurturing from your parent(s) in your life? ☐Y ☐N
6. Have you ever been abandoned or betrayed by a parent figure? ☐Y ☐N
7. Are you living away from your family? ☐Y ☐N
8. Are you pretty isolated and withdrawn socially? ☐Y ☐N
9. Do you spend a lot of time alone? ☐Y ☐N
10. Do you feel lonely most of the time? ☐Y ☐N
11. Are you someone that lacks closeness in your relationships with others? ☐Y ☐N
12. Are your parents divorced? ☐Y ☐N
13. Are you growing up with one parent at home? ☐Y ☐N
14. Would you say the Internet is the main place you connect and communicate with others? ☐Y ☐N
15. Do you spend time in chat rooms on a pretty regular basis? ☐Y ☐N
16. Do you spend more than one hour a day on social networking sites like Facebook? ☐Y ☐N

*If you answered "yes" to three or more questions, this section would be considered a vulnerability.
If you answered "no" to more than 13 questions, this section would be considered a strength.

RELATIONSHIPS IN YOUR LIFE

1. Would you describe yourself as shy? [Y] [N]
2. Do you often feel insecure or anxious in social situations? [Y] [N]
3. Do you struggle getting along with others? [Y] [N]
4. Are you sometimes aggressive with others? [Y] [N]
5. Would others say you have a controlling personality? [Y] [N]
6. Do you often feel irritable with others or do you often get annoyed with small things? [Y] [N]
7. Are you someone with a strong need for intimacy and closeness? [Y] [N]
8. Would you say you are a very emotionally sensitive person? [Y] [N]
9. Would you describe yourself overall as pretty self-absorbed and not really concerned about the feelings of other people? [Y] [N]
10. Would you say the main purpose of sex is personal pleasure? [Y] [N]

*If you answered "yes" to two or more questions, this section would be considered a vulnerability.
If you answered "no" to nine or more questions, this section would be considered a strength.

ACCOUNTABILITY

1. Do you feel uncomfortable talking about things openly in your home or with your family? [Y] [N]
2. Do your parents avoid conversations with you about healthy sexuality? [Y] [N]
3. Do you find yourself keeping a lot of secrets from people you love? [Y] [N]
4. Do you ever use lies to protect yourself? [Y] [N]
5. Do you find yourself not being completely honest with yourself about your life? [Y] [N]
6. Do you have free and easy access to any Internet website with nobody monitoring your use? [Y] [N]
7. Do you connect to the Internet in a private place in the home, where others can't see over your shoulder? [Y] [N]
8. Do you often connect to the Internet late at night? [Y] [N]

*If you answered "yes" to two or more questions, this section would be considered a vulnerability.
If you answered "no" to seven of the eight questions, this section would be considered a strength.

REAL CONNECTIONS

Roughly 20 percent of Americans—about 60 million people—are unhappy with their lives because of loneliness. This is happening throughout the entire Western world. We are starting to see the results of what experts are calling a loneliness epidemic (Marche, 2012).

In an effort to better understand how Americans are connecting to those around them, Harvard University sociologist Dr. Robert Putnam conducted surveys with a group of individuals over a 30 year time period, focusing on people's sense of connection with others and their community. He surveyed things such as card playing, bowling leagues, friends hanging out, family vacations, family dinners, church attendance, and civic participation. By almost every measure, the connectedness of Americans decreased (Putnam, 2000).

Simply put, people are not spending their free time with others as much as they used to. Instead, they're spending it in front of a screen. Dr. Putnam points out: "Between 1965 and 1995, we gained an average of six hours a week in added leisure time, and we spent almost all six of those additional hours watching TV." (Putnum, 2000)

That was a study done more than a decade ago. Do you think we've gotten better since? Nope. It's become a lot worse. Today we have more opportunities than ever to connect with each other through technology and social media, and yet we have an increased lack of actual human connection. According to researchers at Carnegie Mellon University, in 1998 Internet use began coinciding with increased loneliness. Research suggests that, as a society, we have hit the highest level of loneliness recorded and it is profoundly impacting our mental and physical well-being (Science-Daily, 1998).

At the beginning of the twentieth century, 20 percent of adults over 45 years old reported being chronically lonely. By 2010, that number had grown to 35 percent reporting chronic loneliness (Anderson, 2010). That's a 75 percent increase in ten years.

Now let's clarify, there is a difference between loneliness and being alone; they are actually very different. Being alone can be a really good thing—a time to think clearly, uninterrupted; to reinvent ourselves and self-reflect. Loneliness, however, is an empty feeling from not having companionship or friendship. It's a psychological state, not the physical state of being alone.

In other words, you could be in the middle of Times Square on New Year's Eve surrounded by thousands of people and still feel lonely. On the other hand, you could be on a hike in the mountains totally alone and feel completely content with your solitude.

It's important that we feel connected to others and focus on real-life relationships. Did you know that a human baby who is regularly fed and changed, with proper environmental conditions could die from not getting enough human contact? (Benjamin, 2000). It's in our DNA. Social connections are necessary for us to be healthy and happy, just like food, water, and sleep. We are meant to experience life as the social beings we are. And those meaningful social relationships are much more satisfying than the counterfeit comfort of pornog-

raphy. In fact, pornography has been shown to actually cause isolation. Many people who were once outgoing and loved being in social settings became more isolated and socially awkward due to a pornography addiction (Zimbardo & Duncan, 2012).

John Cacioppo, one of the world's leading experts on loneliness, discovered that having more face-to-face interactions decreases loneliness, and that a powerful way to prevent loneliness is to have healthy connections in your life and use your free time to connect with those you care about (Cacioppo, 2008).

The more we connect with others and remove ourselves from isolation, the less desire we will have to turn to an addiction. Over time, our minds will become so engaged and satisfied by connecting with others that our addiction will be forced to take a back seat, and will eventually leave the car.

"So what about technology? Can't it sometimes help us connect more?"

Sure. That's one thing we all enjoy about technology. Let's be honest, social networks like Facebook are pretty awesome. It just depends on how we use technology—and how much we lean on it. For example, if you use a social network to organize an Ultimate Frisbee game, we'd say that's a good way to connect. However, if you turn to a social network instead of playing that Ultimate Frisbee game, then it's feeding your isolation and therefore setting you up for addiction. Although you might have lots of friends on Facebook or Twitter, published research from sociologist Eric Klinenberg has shown that it is the quality, not quantity, of social interaction that best predicts whether or not a person will be lonely.

And get this, 23 percent of Facebook users check in more than five times a day! In the U.S. alone, 58 million people check their social media Web sites more frequently than they eat meals. Many of us now pseudo-communicate through the Internet to have an artificial social experience.

The problem with living our lives online is that we focus less and less on deep connections and meaningful friend-ships, and focus more and more on hollow connections, and that is making us lonelier (Krasnova, Wenninger, Widjaja, & Buxmann, 2013). We are increasingly spend-ing the majority of our interactions with others in front of a screen. The convenience of social-network relationships can make it tempting to think this type of connection with others is just as good and in some cases better than rela-tionships developed face to face. The truth is, it's not.

To help you take a step forward in your recovery, take some time to analyze the connections and relationships in your life. Try to assess whether they are real connections (connections that are meaningful and can lead to true sat-isfaction) or whether they are hollow connections (con-nections that are focused on self-indulgence and mean-ingless discussion).

As you start to remove the hollow connections in your life and replace them with real connections, you'll find your life to be more meaningful and rewarding, which in turn will help fortify you against addiction.

QUICK QUESTION:
Have you felt more isolated or more lonely since you began struggling with your addiction? If so, in what way(s)?

BATTLE STRATEGY #11:

List out some ideas of how you can increase the real connections in your life. Be specific.

(Go to your Battle Strategy in the back of the book on page 233 to answer.)

⭐ ACTION

Pick someone in your life that you haven't made time for in a while—preferably a member of your family. See if you can make extra time to be with them this week.

IT'S ALL ABOUT RELATIONSHIPS

OK, we've talked about the importance of real connections and avoiding hollow connections in our life. Now let's talk about making sure those real connections we do have are healthy.

Most people have no idea that the relationships they have with their parents, siblings, friends, and girlfriend or boyfriend can either help prevent addiction or set them up for addiction. It all comes down to the overall health and quality of those relationships.

In the Fortify Your Relationships Inventory we asked you questions about your relationships. Your responses can help you identify a number of different qualities that could be either strengthening or weakening your relationships—from selfishness and anger to sensitivity and love. We could literally talk for hours about the importance of strong, healthy relationships when trying to quit an addiction, but we promise we won't keep you here that long!

The goal here is to help you recognize potentially unhealthy relationships in your life and help you understand the importance of healing those relationships; we also want to give you a few tips on how to do so.

Healthy relationships are what make us feel fulfilled in life. If we have holes in our relationships, we often try to fill the void with something that makes us instantly feel better, and this fosters addiction.

So what does an unhealthy relationship look like? How do you know if a relationship is unhealthy or healthy?

Recognizing whether a relationship is unhealthy takes being really honest with yourself. Do you often feel anger when you talk with the person? Do you avoid them because you're afraid you might end up fighting? Do you hold your real emotions back when you're in their presence because you're not sure how they'll respond? Do you constantly feel jealous of their accomplishments? Do you find yourself doing things that they've asked you not to do just to get under their skin? Do you struggle to find positive things to say about them?

These unhealthy relationships can be especially difficult when it's with a member of your family, since it's much easier to distance yourself if the other person doesn't sleep under the same roof as you.

The thing is, family relationships are the most important relationships we'll ever have. Friends and casual acquaintances will come and go in our lives, but our family will always be connected to us. We can promise you that learning to heal and improve your most important relationships earlier will save you a lot of headache and heartache later on.

So what does a healthy relationship look like? Let's review the basic relationship skills that, if practiced, will make life a lot more enjoyable.

1. Focus on others' strengths rather than their weaknesses: Look, we all have weaknesses, right? Nobody likes to constantly hear about their own weaknesses, and when they do it can be pretty hard on a relationship. Instead, let's focus our time and energies on others' strengths and what they do well. You can't imagine the difference this simple shift can make in a struggling relationship.

2. Serve: Foster the desire to serve others around you and make time to perform service. Every minute you spend thinking about others and doing something for them is another minute where your brain is detoxing and rewiring itself back to where you want it to be.

3. Be completely honest: Nothing destroys a healthy relationship faster than dishonesty. If those you care about can't trust you, you're going to have a really hard time cultivating healthy relationships. Stick to the truth and that's it. Don't allow yourself to stretch, hide, dodge, avoid, spin, or manipulate anything when it comes to the truth.

4. Say you're sorry: This isn't always easy, but it can be one of the most powerful tools in healing a relationship. Many people don't apologize because they think that it looks like a weakness—a failure. Yet people also say that when they hear others apologize to them they see it as a sign of strength and great character. Why is that? Why do we look at the ability to apologize as a good thing from others and a bad thing from ourselves? The truth is that it is not a sign of

weakness but a profound sign of strength, humility, and good intent. Try it out. See what happens.

5. Forgive often: Healthy relationships thrive when each individual is quick to forgive the other for things that they have done. Holding on to past offenses greatly limits your ability to maintain a good relationship. You need to learn to let things go. We promise that you will be happier if you do.

6. Open up: Communication is key for any great relationship. Open up and talk about small things like how your day went, as well as bigger things like your hopes and fears. This open communication will lay the foundation for a vibrant and rich relationship.

There you have it—a pretty good snapshot of what a healthy relationship looks like. Work on one tip at a time until you have successfully implemented all six into the most important relationships in your life.

Imagine having better relationships with everyone—your parents, your siblings, your coworkers, and maybe a significant other. As you practice having healthy relationships in one area of your life—like with your family— you are establishing good habits that will help you have healthy relationships in other areas, such as with friends or a girlfriend or boyfriend.

Picture those healthy relationships being a part of your life for good. Hold on to those images. This is something that you can look forward to. In the meantime, find the things you can start doing today to improve and possibly repair the relationships around you.

In turn, as you fortify your relationships, pornography will become less and less alluring. You will be engaged in something that is much more satisfying than pornography—healthy relationships with real people.

BATTLE STRATEGY #12:

Which relationships in your life are you going to focus on? What specific actions are you going to take to strengthen them?

(Go to your Battle Strategy in the back of the book on page 233 to answer.)

⭐ ACTION

Within the next few days, find an opportunity to serve someone close to you. It could be as simple as making the bed of someone in your family, setting the table without being asked, helping your friend with his or her homework, or offering to tend your siblings while your parents go on a date.

TIME TO GET SERIOUS

Now that we've explored the importance of healthy relationships, we are going to revisit an earlier topic: accountability. Why? Because it's that important!

You need to realize that trying to fight an addiction without sharing the problem with someone you trust is kind of like asking a doctor to heal you without sharing your symptoms. If you are not open and honest with others, you are more vulnerable to addiction.

Secrecy is addiction's favorite fuel. Keeping secrets aids the addiction because it masks bad habits from others and

allows an addict to feel like they are getting away with
their behaviors without having serious consequences.
Addicts often don't realize that secrecy isn't a long-term
solution. Many times they think that keeping their addiction secret is something that can go on forever. They convince themselves that they will never get caught. The
truth is, addiction always surfaces. It's not a question of
whether others will find out, but when.

Those close to the addict will eventually realize something is up—even if they can't put their finger on what is
wrong. Your family will wonder. Your friends will notice
things. So it's to your advantage to take control of the situation and be the one to open up rather than wait until
your addiction tells on you.

It seems reasonable that you might want to shield your
family from the pain of knowing you have an addiction,
right? After all, if you don't tell them, maybe you can
spare them the hurt. This may seem to work for a while.
Your girlfriend or boyfriend or brother or sister or parents or friends may be clueless at first, and they may seem
better off because of it.

However, they will start to feel the distance and lack of
connection to you. If you've seen that pattern begin to
develop, maybe it's time to make some changes. If you
want to feel close with your loved ones, honesty and
openness are key. Communication is a necessary ingredient in every healthy relationship. Imagine what it would
feel like to have no secrets.

Imagine having a relationship with someone where they
know everything about you and they still love you uncon-
ditionally. Sounds great, doesn't it?

Of course it does. And it's possible, but it will take some
hard work.

Some of you might be thinking, "They're going to be mad," or "I'm ashamed of what they will think." We want you to know that in almost every case, as you open up to people who are trustworthy and sincerely show that you need support, you'll find that many around you are willing to help.

Pornography has driven you apart from people who care about you. We are trying to counterbalance that force—to encourage you to move back in the other direction, to see your parents and other trusted adults as allies, not opponents.

That courageous moment where you sit down with a parent or trusted adult in full honesty could become a huge turning point in your recovery. Trust us! Being open and honest will help you tackle this addiction so that you don't have to live with skeletons in your closet anymore, and you won't have to keep this secret from others.

Because it can be difficult to take this step, we've come up with nine tips on how to build the courage to share what you're going through and have a positive experience when you do.

1. Realize that you are not your addiction. It is not you; it is something that has infiltrated your life and you are taking the steps needed to get rid of it.

2. Think about the fact that you are reading this book and recognize the progress that you have made so far. Having the willpower to recover is a big deal. By reading this far into this book, you've shown that you are dedicated to changing.

3. Select an accountability partner who is trustworthy and will be a good support. We recommend opening up to a trusted adult who cares about your future and would be willing to help.

4. Make sure when you plan to have your first discussion with your accountability partner that you have time to adequately address the issue. You may need an hour or two or three. Just make sure that there is nothing in the way of your ability to get everything out in this discussion.

5. Only share details that are relevant to your recovery and that you are comfortable sharing. Your accountability partner may not need to know every gritty specific detail.

6. Be calm, patient, and understanding of the other person's reaction. Detach yourself from the addiction; don't defend it.

7. Have a humble attitude and communicate your willingness to change and work toward a solution. Recognize that you may need help.

8. Consider setting up a weekly check-in on your progress. Have your accountability partner look into Internet filtration systems or accountability software that will help keep you committed.

9. Share your Battle Strategy, goals, and potential vulnerabilities so your accountability partner can be fully aware of how to assist your recovery. If you don't yet have a plan, create one together.

Many have found that having an accountability partner is a solid motivation to quit the addiction for good. Don't underestimate the value of having a trustworthy, positive support that you can speak with concerning this issue.

QUICK QUESTION:
What do you need from an accountability partner?

BATTLE STRATEGY #13:

Refer back to the list of possible accountability partners you created earlier. Map out a plan to approach one of these individuals based on the tips we just discussed.

(Go to your Battle Strategy in the back of the book on page 234 to create your plan.)

⭐ ACTION

After finishing Battle Strategy #13, approach the person you've chosen and ask them to be your accountability partner. If needed, use the script below as a guide.

Hey, can I talk to you for a second? I trust you a lot and that's why I am talking to you now. I think I need your help with something that I've been struggling with. I want you to understand that I have tried to deal with it on my own for some time but feel that to truly overcome this I will need your help and possibly the help of others.

I've been struggling with pornography, and after learning that it can be just as addictive as other drugs, I realized that I couldn't overcome it on my own. So I started the *Fortify* program—a program developed for teens struggling with an addiction to pornography—and it has helped me understand the importance of getting someone like you involved. I feel like I need to be accountable to somebody, and I'm hoping that you will be willing to be that person. Will you be my accountability partner? It would help if we got together at least once a week to talk about my challenges and progress as well as discuss ideas on how I can continue to improve. It might be good if you also monitored my Internet usage using accountability software to help me stay focused.

I may eventually invite others to help as well to strengthen my support and chances of recovery. This is a very personal issue and I trust that you will keep this between us until I am comfortable opening up to others. Thank you for listening and understanding. That means a lot to me and I already feel more confident in my ability to beat this with your help.

CHECK-IN

Great work on getting this far! By fortifying yourself and your relationships, you're taking steps to eliminate the darkness in your life by filling your life with light through healthy activities and habits. Your path out of this addiction is likely becoming clearer, and there's nothing better than being able to finally see some light at the end of the tunnel—a tunnel you may have been traveling down for far too long.

And though you're starting to see an end in sight, don't let that distract you from the importance of exercising the strategies that have brought you this far. Consistently using those strategies will carry you the rest of the way.

So let's check in and see how you're doing with one of the most crucial strategies: securing your home base.

How's that going so far? Have you reinforced your base by eliminating possible triggers or avoiding specific encounters? What steps have you taken to make your home base a place where you can't lose? Have you reviewed your personal battle strategy and the list of ideas you wanted to implement? What kind of impact has it had on your addiction so far? Are there things that have been neglected and still need attention?

It does take time to make things secure, and often you won't see all the holes in your base without falling a few times. But once you're aware of those chinks in your armor, there are no more excuses.

What we've found to be most difficult about implementing this strategy is simply implementing it. So, if you still need to find new friends who can be supportive and a positive influence during your recovery, do it! If you still haven't eliminated those TV shows and programs that usually set you up for a setback, do it! If you haven't installed a filtration system on your Internet-enabled devices, do it! If you haven't made adjustments to the types of music, games, and media you're consuming, do it! We know what we need to do; however, it's the doing that we often procrastinate, hoping things will improve without actually having to improve them.

Don't forget what we said earlier: for those Fighters serious about victory, securing your home base is essential for a successful recovery.

CHAPTER SIX

FORTIFY YOUR WORLD

FORTIFY YOUR WORLD

FORTIFY YOUR WORLD INVENTORY

Instructions: The following inventory is a way of helping you explore the potential contributors to addiction. Each question comes from a research study that correlates or connects this issue to online addiction of some kind.

Rather than searching for one single cause of addiction, the focus here is the root system that underlies addiction and explores both areas of vulnerability and areas of strength.

To score your inventory, count the number of times you answered "yes" in each section and compare that total number to the scoring metric at the bottom of each section to find out whether that area would be considered a vulnerability or a strength in your life.

MENTAL CONSUMPTION		
1. Do you watch a lot of TV?	Y	N
2. Would you say you spend a lot of time online every week (more than 3 hours/day on average)?	Y	N
3. Do you get online multiple times a day?	Y	N
4. When you get online, do you spend a lot of time in one sitting?	Y	N
5. Did you start browsing the Internet before age 9?	Y	N
6. Would you say you use the Internet mostly for having fun?	Y	N
7. Do you play computer or video games nearly every day?	Y	N
8. Do you find yourself consistently looking for more mental and visual stimulation?	Y	N
9. Are you sometimes hyperactive?	Y	N

*If you answered "yes" to two or more questions, this section would be considered a vulnerability.
If you answered "no" to eight or more questions, this section would be considered a strength.

PRODUCTIVITY

1. Do you often feel bored? ☐Y ☐N
2. Do you prefer having nothing to do rather than being busy? ☐Y ☐N
3. Does your family believe that school is not that important? ☐Y ☐N
4. If you're attending school, are you failing any of your classes? ☐Y ☐N
5. Do you sometimes skip school? ☐Y ☐N
6. Do you often get overwhelmed by tasks and find yourself giving up early
to do something more enjoyable? ☐Y ☐N
7. Do you hate keeping a schedule or routine? ☐Y ☐N
8. Do you use your free time to do things that are not important or necessary? ☐Y ☐N
9. Do you find it hard to concentrate in class or when someone is giving a lecture? ☐Y ☐N
10. Have you ever been diagnosed with ADHD? ☐Y ☐N

*If you answered "yes" to three or more questions, this section would be considered a vulnerability.
If you answered "no" to eight or more questions, this section would be considered a strength.

STRESS IN YOUR LIFE

1. Do you currently have high amounts of stress? ☐Y ☐N
2. To your knowledge, is your family's current financial situation difficult? ☐Y ☐N
3. Do you feel that you have a stressful shortage of money for your own needs? ☐Y ☐N
4. Have you had a sudden increase of stress in your life lately? ☐Y ☐N
5. Are there relationships in your life that cause you stress, such as with
family, peers, or teachers? ☐Y ☐N
6. Does your family often argue? ☐Y ☐N
7. Do you feel that the stress in your life is uncontrollable and never ending? ☐Y ☐N
8. Do you feel pain or discomfort in your body related to stressful things in you
life? ☐Y ☐N
9. Would you say your physical health is poor right now? ☐Y ☐N
10. Do you feel helpless when it comes to managing your anxiety,
boredom, loneliness, sadness, or depression? ☐Y ☐N
11. Are mildly difficult situations incredibly hard to deal with? ☐Y ☐N
12. Is it common for you to try and escape or avoid uncomfortable feelings
(anxiety, boredom, sadness) some way? ☐Y ☐N

*If you answered "yes" to three or more questions, this section would be considered a vulnerability.
If you answered "no" to 10 or more questions, this section would be considered a strength.

STAYING IN SHAPE MENTALLY

Our society pays a lot of attention to how we eat, how we exercise, and how much physical rest we get. Unfortunately, there is much less awareness of what we take in and consume mentally and emotionally.

Just as what we take into our bodies has a large impact on us, so too does what we take into our minds. In the same way that physical rest makes a difference in how our bodies feel and function, making sure you have some time to rest mentally can be essential to your recovery. We are stronger against addiction when we are functioning with a healthy amount of mental exercise and rest. When we are mentally and emotionally worn out, we are more likely to give in to an urge.

Remember the Big Three we explored when we talked about living a healthy life—sleep, exercise, and diet? We will apply those same principles to our mental well-being. We'll call them mental rest, mental exercise, and mental diet.

Like the food we take into our bodies, the ideas, information, and images we take into our minds help shape who we are, how we feel, and what we do. When we allow harmful messages or images to invade our minds, it affects our brain and our life as a whole.

But we don't have to tell you that. You've felt the effects of harmful media in your life. You've seen it transform your perceptions for the worse and influence the way you behave. You've become dependent on this kind of media; and because you enjoyed this mental junk food, it has likely pushed you to isolate yourself from interactions with others.

On the other hand, media that is inspiring or educational is a mentally nutritious diet that nourishes and energizes you. This kind of media teaches you something or motivates and encourages you to do things that will make your life more fulfilling. This kind of learning provides support for your mental and emotional well-being.

A good way to start improving your mental fitness is to just start to pay attention to how the different kinds of media you consume influence you personally. Remember, when you fill your life and mind with the good stuff, there will eventually be no place for the junk.

Not only is it important to focus on what media we consume, it is also important to regulate how much we consume.

More and more people are taking their media consumption to an extreme—filling every free moment possible with some kind of entertainment or another, and those who suffer from a pornography addiction are particularly vulnerable. Many people facing pornography addiction also struggle with an overall obsession with media. Do you find yourself always needing to have some media stimulation? Pornography aside, we can become hooked on media stimulation, sacrificing our schoolwork and relationships in the pursuit of getting a media buzz.

Here are some signs that you need to adjust your media diet:
• You woke up this morning with a cell phone clutched in your hand.
• You interrupt a night with a good friend to update your Facebook status.
• You prefer texting to a human interaction.
• You tune out of a conversation to quickly check your email.
• You feel completely lost without your phone or gadget.
• The TV has to be on when you're at home for you to feel comfortable.

- You can't hang out with others without watching a movie or playing video games.
- You check out status updates while you're sitting at a red light.
- You text while driving.
- You texted your mom to pass the potatoes at dinner.

Let's hope none of us are guilty of that last one.

Media overload is becoming more and more common and has been associated with a host of problems, including attention difficulties, low grades, impaired sleep, obesity, and withdrawal from family life. When a person is always plugged in, it is hard to become free from pornography addiction.

The National Day of Unplugging (NDU) was recently created by Reboot, whose mission is to encourage "hyper-connected and frequently frantic people of all backgrounds to re-embrace moments and even days of rest from media"(Reboot, 2010). Its founders encourage people to "shut down your computer. Turn off your cell phone. Stop the constant emailing, texting, Tweeting, and Facebooking to take time to notice the world around you. Connect with loved ones. Nurture your health. Get outside. Find silence. Give back. Eat together."

This kind of rest from digital over-stimulus can be done by yourself or with others. One group called Unplug and Reconnect has the motto: "Love Technology... Love People More." Google Chairman Eric Schmidt urges people to unplug at least one hour a day. "Take one hour a day and turn that thing off. Take your eyes off that screen and look into the eyes of those around you. Have a conversation, a real conversation" (Musil, 2012). The idea is simply to help people become more aware of our relationship with technology, and create a relationship that reflects the balance we want.

To make sure you are in control of your media consumption you might want to try finding some regular "unplug and reconnect" time for you—unplugging for a few hours and finding a special tech-free time of day when you can enjoy a meal without interruptions, or focus on family or a friend. Or you can choose one electronic device to turn off for the day, such as your TV or computer. Find times when you can leave your phone behind, if only for short periods at a time, like when you go to the gym, to the store, or to church.

Does this sound difficult? Don't let it be. This is about finding and striking a healthy balance and enjoying media in a healthy way. There's a lot of flexibility in how you do this.

For someone struggling with a pornography addiction, it can be extremely important to limit the overall time spent watching TV, playing video games, and using computers for entertainment. As committed as you may feel to avoiding certain sites, research studies have proven the more hours you spend browsing the Internet alone, the more likely you are to continue your addiction. For the foreseeable future—until you are truly free—consider some courageous limits.

QUICK QUESTION:
Which activities or persons in your life are contributing to a healthy mental diet and which are contributing to an unhealthy mental diet?

BATTLE STRATEGY #14:

What actions are you going to take to improve your own mental diet? Be specific.

(Go to your Battle Strategy in the back of the book on page 234 to answer.)

⭐ ACTION

If you want to really be brave, consider a mini Social Media (Facebook, Twitter, Instagram etc.) vacation. That's right. Give up Social Media for a day, a week, a weekend, a month. Does the very thought of disconnecting from Social Media fill you with dread? Don't let it. We're not saying to get rid of your account completely; we're just suggesting you step away for a little while.

WORKING HARD OR HARDLY WORKING

Have you ever met someone who never has any obligations? Someone who does whatever they feel like in the moment? Some people like living without any schedules—kind of floating here and there, showing up for something if they remember.

While this may work for some people, there are risks that come from living this way. One of the risks is that a lack of schedule and routine makes someone more vulnerable to addiction. When we are idle we can fall into damaging habits. Not cool.

A laid-back attitude appears cool on the surface, but an idle person is just opening the door for the next urge to come and tell them what to do.

However, if you're preoccupied with more important things, urges to view pornography don't have much space in your schedule. Being actively involved in meaningful, productive things makes it easier for the brain to remain mentally and emotionally focused on healthy behaviors.

Bottom line: how you structure your time can make a big difference in your ability to combat pornography addiction.

Why would it make such a difference? Let's talk about that.

First of all, nothing will bring you more satisfaction than staying productive. Your self-esteem will improve, and you will feel more capable and accomplished.

Work can be a powerful tool for any recovery—and any life. People who get actively involved in learning, working, and serving others have a leg up on achieving a healthy lifestyle. All of this may be hard to understand at first—especially in the middle of this addiction. You might be wondering, "Why work toward anything when I can feel completely satisfied here next to my computer?"

Virgil Stucker, a psychologist who has spent his whole career helping people recover, said the following: "Every day, whether or not you are facing some kind of emotional challenge, you need to awaken into a world that you know needs you. You need to finish that day knowing that you have contributed—so no matter how ill you are, you need to get up knowing you can help." (Stucker, 2013)

What can you do to contribute? How can you be more productive and avoid being idle? If you have never really been into planning, how do you start? Do you have to go out and get an expensive planner? Not necessarily. The main point is to commit yourself to having some general structure, schedule, and routine to your day.

Here are a few ideas to consider:
- Make a to-do list in the morning and do your best to accomplish it before you go to bed.
- Use a calendar.
- Get involved in your school or community. Have somewhere to go and volunteer.
- Do what you say you're going to do.
- Be where you say you're going to be.
- Always be on time.
- Seek out opportunities to improve your talents and skills.
- Set a time to go to bed and stick to it.
- Get up earlier than you need to and do something that wouldn't normally get done.
- Plan ahead.

If you're willing to do these things, the details of what constructive goals you accomplish will work themselves out. So are you willing? Trust us. It will pay off later. Now get to work!

BATTLE STRATEGY #15:

What changes are you going to make in your life to stay busy and be more productive?

(Go to your Battle Strategy in the back of the book on page 235 to answer.)

ACTION

To help you organize your time, find some way to plan out your next week. If you want to get a calendar and schedule, go for it. Several pieces of paper stapled together can work fine as well. Lay out the next seven days in order, and write down everything you have coming up in those days. Add more than just scheduled appointments by including things like the time of day you are going to wake up and go to bed, time to spend working on a hobby, and time to visit a good friend. If you feel like your days are still not productive enough, find things to add to your schedule.

LIGHTENING THE STRESS LOAD

Okay, in the last section we talked about being productive and how filling your time with good activities can decrease vulnerability for addiction. Now we want to talk about how being too busy and stressed out can lead you to a similar outcome. What we hope for you to find is a balance between the two.

When it comes to dealing with stressful situations, there are two conversations that are important to have, and both are connected to addiction:

1. The overall amount of stress in our lives
2. How we respond to that stress

Let's dive into number one. The reasons we are so stressed out are no mystery. Everywhere you look, there's another example of the "speeding up" of life—instant communication, obsessions with efficiency, and overly crammed schedules that pack in as much as possible. Our society's fast-paced lifestyle has been connected to all sorts of problems—from depression and anxiety to addiction.

Here's the good news: there are ways to slow down the pace and manage the craziness of everyday life; ways to simplify; ways to not spread ourselves too thin. The varieties of adjustments that can be made are endless—from small adjustments to major changes. Go ahead and take a good, hard look at the amount of things on your plate that are causing you stress.

As you decrease your stress level, you also strengthen yourself against addiction. This doesn't always mean doing less however. Sometimes stress comes from not doing enough of the activities that matter most. For instance, when you have an assignment from school or a responsibility at home, if you ignore that—even to relax— it will likely increase stress.

Isn't that funny? Sometimes relaxing—the very thing we think will reduce stress—can actually increase stress, especially if we are neglecting responsibility.

On the other hand, when you prioritize accomplishing important tasks, such as finding a job, improving a relationship, or taking care of something that needs to get done—even if all you can take are small steps—you will feel the stress lighten.

Having fun or playing can also help you reconnect with the best part of who you are and help you see yourself as a whole person again. It also helps you connect to others, which makes building a support group much easier. Bottom line, if there are healthy ways to decrease stress in

your life, take advantage of them! Easing those pressures can help decrease the intensity of urges.

If we stop the conversation here, however, we miss the most exciting part, which brings us to our second topic: how we respond to stress.

Have you ever met someone who is calm and chill, even when faced with tons of stress? Individuals who have developed the mental capacity to not shift into "stress mode" are much safer from the threat of addiction.

How do you get there? Well, the skills you're already starting to practice from Basic Training are a good start. You know how we talked about stepping back and watching the urges swell and eventually subside? That same skill can be applied to other stressful things that happen, such as feeling frustrated or angry with your sister, getting behind on a big assignment in school, or feeling anxious because things aren't happening the way you want.

It takes courage to do this, but it is the beginning of the end in your battle for freedom. When things start to feel a little crazy, remember this: as long as we're running away from the stressful things in our life, we're not only fighting a losing battle, but we are also feeding the addiction itself.

This skill is just one of many healthy ways to deal with stress. Here are a few more that others have found to be very helpful when handling stress.

1. Talk about it: Often the best way to handle a stressful situation is calmly discussing it with someone. Whether it's a parent or a friend, finding someone to talk with can help you see a situation for what it really is.

2. Laugh it off: I'm sure you've heard that laugh-

ter is the great healer to many stressful or difficult situations. There's actually a scientific explanation for this. Did you know that when you laugh you increase the oxygen supply to your lungs, which stimulates the production of endorphins, a hormone that produces feelings of euphoria? In other words, it makes you feel good.

3. Exercise: Burning off when you're feeling stressed can do wonders for your life, not to mention the additional endorphins exercise releases in your brain. Check this out: According to research done at the University of British Columbia, Vancouver, 20 to 30 minutes of exercise at least three times a week can lower a person's stress levels (Van Praugg et. al., 1999).

4. Get real: Accept yourself for who you really are. Learn to manage your strengths and weaknesses. Stop putting yourself down for past mistakes. Learn from them—then put them behind you.

5. Think positively: When life gets hard and things don't seem to be working out, it's easy to have a negative outlook on life. Choosing to adopt a good attitude and positive perspective can be a huge help in keeping stress levels at bay.

It's important to accept that life brings both sorrow and joy. Applying these skills can help you navigate, listen to, and learn from stressful moments. So take a deep breath and go out there knowing that feelings of anxiety or stress, just like an urge, will pass. If you learn to manage your stress in a healthy way, you'll find that it actually starts to decrease and your ability to stay cool, calm, and collected in a difficult situation will increase.

QUICK QUESTION:
How is your stress level right now? Do you feel like your level of stress is contributing to your addiction? Can you identify where those stresses are coming from?

BATTLE STRATEGY #16:

List the three biggest stresses in your life right now and how you plan on responding to those stresses in a healthy way.

(Go to your Battle Strategy in the back of the book on page 235 to answer.)

 **ACTION**

Call up a good friend tonight to talk. If you want to bring up the things that are causing you stress, go for it. If not, that's OK. Sometimes the simple act of talking with a good friend is helpful enough.

FORTIFY YOUR LIFE: RECAP

Well done! You've just worked through different areas of your life that have been shown in various research studies to set people up for addiction. More than simply training for an immediate battle, you're now laying the ground-work for a much broader recovery and a much deeper freedom. We're excited!

You may not feel like you can leave pornography behind forever quite yet. But how about dedicating some extra care to how well you sleep or what you eat? What about your level of exercise? Or improving the relationships in your life? Even if you can't walk away from pornography yet, you can walk toward other changes in your life that can strengthen you. In a sense, every moment becomes a chance to move toward or away from this addiction.

To this point, you've been developing your own personal Battle Strategy. You've made decisions about some things to adjust now, and others to adjust later. With the skills you're gaining and practicing, you're becoming more and more prepared to face this—and beat it. Ultimately, all this groundwork centers on making adjustments to help you realize your full potential.

If you can begin to make these adjustments and you're serious about them, this addiction's days may be numbered because it can't withstand a truly healthy, vibrant life. Pornography addiction only survives in emotional darkness and emptiness. As you fill your life up with good stuff, it doesn't have a chance!

From uplifting books, music, movies, hobbies, and activities, to more connection with friends and family and renewed spiritual practices, you have lots of options for positive and healthy ways to focus your time and energy. Filling your life with this kind of light will mean the darkness will have far less opportunity to bully you. Ultimately, this is about building a life that's so good that pornography becomes a nuisance, rather than a temptation.

Bottom line: rather than simply trying to resist pornography, creating healthy habits and embracing a life that is full of things that are far better than this addiction is the real secret to recovery.

CHECK-IN

Hey, you're making great progress. You've just finished a very comprehensive look at your life. You probably saw some areas of your life that you felt confident and strong about. You also probably recognized areas of your life that were setting you up for addictive behaviors. Pinpointing those areas that need improvement is the first step in fixing the problem.

Speaking of fixing the problem, how are you doing with tracking your battles? Are you using your Battle Tracker? If you just answered that question with a "no," then you are missing out on an extremely powerful tool that will greatly increase your chances of reaching true recovery.

If you have diligently been using your Battle Tracker, what patterns have you noticed? Is there a certain time of day that you most often struggle? Is there a theme to where you are when you have a setback? Have you been able to increase the time between setbacks? What changes have you implemented in your life due to what you have learned from your Battle Tracker?

Again, gathering this information about your addiction can give you an advantage over the enemy. Over time, you will be able to recognize trends and patterns that lead you to using, and eventually you'll be able to avoid using altogether.

HAPTER SEVEN >> RISE AND RISE AGAIN

WE DO HARD THINGS

Whenever we begin something new, it's easy to feel excited and gung-ho, whether for a new school year, a new job, or a new relationship.

Then life happens! As time passes, feelings of newness naturally go away, excitement can settle, and other feelings can arise—including feelings we don't always like. School can start to get hard or boring; a new job can start to feel dull, and a relationship can get challenging as two people figure out how (and whether) to love each other when the initial excitement starts to fade.

Something similar can happen while moving through your own recovery. At this point, you've spent some real time working with *Fortify*—assuming you haven't been rushing too fast! Maybe you felt some excitement as you started this and dove into some different trainings that hopefully felt exciting.

As you've learned new things about the brain, tried out new tactics, learned new techniques, and created your own Battle Strategy, we've also talked repeatedly about the many reasons for hope in what lies ahead for you. As you finish this program and get back to your regular routine and normal feelings, is any of this stuff going to really matter and really stick? It's worth talking about. As the newness of what you've heard dies away, what will all of this mean for your life? With sections on training and overall strategy behind us, now it's time to talk more directly about what this stuff looks like in the messy, crazy-hard, frustrating, up-and-down experiences of life.

After years of addiction, someone might look at *Fortify* and think, "Do these guys know how incredibly hard it is to even start turning away from this stuff? Do they realize I still can hardly go a week, or a day, without using?" Maybe you've tried some of the skills from basic training and it's still hard. You're still having a tough time. If that's where you're at, then listen up: the people who built this program know what you're going through. We know what this is like for you—not only from reading books, but also from our own lives.

What this means is we are not naive about how hard this can be for you. We absolutely realize how hard this is and how difficult it can be to even move just a few steps in the right direction! That's why we're not saying, "Just try harder and this will all go away," or "Just finish this program and your life will be changed instantly!" No— we celebrated at the beginning because you were brave enough to start something new. We will celebrate at the end for the same reason; but the real celebration will come a year from now, three years from now, and ten years from now, when you will see the true benefits of living a porn-free lifestyle.

If your desire to stop using is small and inconsistent today, don't worry. It can grow. If your ability to stay clean is weak, that's why we're doing this together. Trust what we're sharing, we're doing this with you. Trust the tactics, tips, and ideas we're giving you as well as the Battle Strategy you're creating for yourself. Trust the process. The process of backing away from pornography is similar to stepping away and tapering off other things your body has a love-hate relationship with. It takes time for your brain to get used to life without illegal drugs or cigarettes, too. If you stay away long enough, the body will read- just, detox, and start to crave better things. Every moment that you are working on real relationships is another moment of deeper healing. Every moment that your mind is focused on uplifting ideas is another moment of brain restoration.

Don't try to fight tomorrow's battles today. Take one moment at a time.

As we keep telling you, you have so many reasons to be hopeful! The more your brain begins to strengthen and create new neural pathways, the less the old ones get used. And the less they get used, the more they begin to atrophy—and the more you are able to heal. Give this process enough time, and choosing not to use will become just as much of a habit as using once was!

In order to get there, though, as we've said all along, you're going to have to fight. A part of this comes down to being tough. This didn't start out as an equal fight; rather than starting this program on a level playing field, you come to it as a prisoner in chains seeking to rebel.

Your freedom and peace is worth any sacrifice—any price. As a group of Fighters, one of our mottos is "We do hard things." During your battle toward recovery, you will become another kind of person—someone that doesn't just run from pain anymore, that doesn't crumble in the face of intense urges, someone that endures, who feels resistance but keeps pushing forward.

This person may feel a long way off—but believe us, it's your future if you want it.

QUICK QUESTION:
Do you ever get frustrated or worn out in facing this addiction—worried that you'll never get to better place? How long has it been since you first started trying to walk away from pornography? How does it feel right now for you?

⭐ ACTION

Write down our motto, "We do hard things!" on a piece of paper and pin it up somewhere you'll see it every day to remind you that you can do this.

TURBULENCE IN THE BRAIN

Throughout your recovery you're going to come across moments and messages that challenge your determination for freedom. You're going to face fatigue and unexpected attacks against everything you're working for. At times, you're even going to fall.

In spite of all these new tools, personal skills, and battle strategies, cravings will still come and urges will still arise. Why is it that urges can hit right when you're trying to make progress?

One big reason for this is your brain does not change as fast as your lifestyle and environment can; even if you've made a commitment to go in a certain direction, your neural pathways still represent the directions you went yesterday and the days before. This means the body inevitably lags behind your awareness a couple of steps and creates some resistance.

So it's time to buckle up. Cigarette smokers working toward recovery describe the week after they quit smoking as "hell week." As your brain is adjusting and reshaping itself to a new setting and new habits, the physiological changes will slowly take hold—but not without a fight.

Once again, the body's patterns don't change easily. For a smoker who has conditioned his or her brain to crave nicotine for years, you can't expect that brain to suddenly be happy when it's gone.

It has taken time, many decisions, and actions to get your body and brain where they are now. And it will take similar amounts of effort, if not more, to move it in the other direction. This doesn't mean you will get to the point where provocative images are suddenly not arousing; instead, it means your brain will get to the point where you have the strength to decide whether or not you want to view them.

It's not only physical resistance that can cause challenges. Another level of turbulence can arise from tempting rationalizations—things we think or say to help us feel better about something we're not proud of. We convince ourselves that something is not a big deal, so we don't have to face an unpleasant reality. You know what we're talking about:

"One look won't hurt."
"Just a little will be OK."
"I will change eventually."
"As long as I stay away from the really bad stuff, I'll be OK."
"I can stop any time I want to."
"I will stop when I get a girlfriend or boyfriend."
"I will stop when I start college/have less stress in my life."
"At least I am not into drugs."
"This is the last time."
"I will just keep it a secret. No one will ever need to know."

You've heard some of these before—maybe in your own head. While they seem different, each of them contains the same basic idea: "What I'm about to do is OK. It is justified. It is understandable. Go ahead—DO IT!"

Simply put, by rationalizing we are actually lying to ourselves—tricking ourselves into believing that there's no harm in what we're about to do. Deep down, of course, we know this isn't true.

These small justifications can actually become a huge barrier. Very often, a binge begins with just one look. Allowing yourself to justify a decision that can lead you into the addiction cycle is like surrendering the battle before it even begins.

In order to maintain control during those moments of turbulence, you need to practice holding on to your seat and focusing on the final destination. Don't take your mind off your long-term goals. Every time a thought enters your mind that minimizes your true desires and tries to convince you that a bad decision is not a big deal, remember where you came from, recognize how far you've come, and stay focused on your desired destination. Resist the temptation to embrace a lie to feel OK about some instant pseudo-pleasure.

Think back to Basic Training where we taught you a powerful strategy: S.T.A.R. Using S.T.A.R. can help you take a step back and respond to temptations in a healthy way. Finding an anchor—something or someone you love more than your addiction—can help you find the motivation and strength to endure the turbulence in your brain.

Of course, even with work, pornography withdrawal will mean some turbulence and aftershocks in your brain. This is no different than the withdrawal that comes from tobacco, alcohol, or other drugs. Similar to moving a river, the channels in your brain will take some time to redirect. Be patient. Stick with it. If you stay strong during those challenging moments, you can't lose!

QUICK QUESTION:
What internal messages do you struggle with most?

PORN PROPAGANDA

Sometimes it's hard to know what is true and what is not when listening to the messages coming at us every day in the media. While watching TV or reading a blog, you'll come across messages that seem to contradict everything we've been teaching you in this book. If this hasn't happened to you already, it will.

You hear or read things like:

"This is natural and normal behavior."
"Everybody is doing it."
"It feels good, so how bad can it be?"
"It is not hurting anyone."

One old war tactic used to involve having military planes fly over enemy lines to drop leaflets with messages designed to create fear and persuade people to give up. As a fighter, don't be surprised when the same thing happens to you. The porn industry does this today.

If we're not careful, this propaganda can shake the very foundation upon which we are building our recovery. It can make us question our own commitments and core desires to the point where we might even start to believe those bogus messages, despite all we have learned.

Don't let that happen!

Remember, it took more than 40 years from the time research came out against smoking for mainstream media and pop culture to finally recognize that it was harmful. Only recently have we started to see anti-smoking messages on TV, movies, and the Internet. It might take another 30 or even 50 years for us to see the same thing regarding the harmful effects of pornography, so don't hold your breath.

Like we said earlier, when it comes to shifting public perception, things don't often move fast. You're going to need to be prepared for these counter attacks if you want to succeed in your recovery. You can do this by educating yourself through books, articles, documentaries, and other reputable sources. This knowledge will help you recognize when a message from the media is true or false, helpful or harmful. Then, when you come across a false message, you will be better prepared to reject it and move past it.

Now we're not saying that all media is bad. Of course it isn't. We cannot begin to list all of the great benefits we enjoy thanks to advancements in media messaging. Nor are we saying that all media is good. Like most things, it simply depends on the messages being delivered. Some are incredibly helpful and uplifting, while others reek of falsehood and can be quite damaging if we let them.

Go to Fight the New Drug's resource page to find materials and organizations that can offer helpful information.

By learning how to decipher the messages that often force themselves into our lives and try to derail our progress, we will be far more prepared to withstand them and stay strong amid opposition.

QUICK QUESTION:
What messages from the media about sexuality do you hear most often? Why do you think people buy into false messages so easily?

⭐ ACTION

Pay close attention to the media influences around you in the next 24 hours. Notice the subtle messages you come across in TV programs and commercials, billboards, magazines, radio, music, advertisements, etc., that relate to sexuality. Identify which messages you accept and which messages you reject.

NAVIGATING THE EBB AND FLOW OF YOUR OWN DESIRE

The Bay of Fundy, found on the eastern coast of Canada between New Brunswick and Nova Scotia, is known for having the highest tide range in the world. In a matter of 13 hours, the tide can rise 53 feet and then recede back to its original depth. At times, our own desires can feel a bit like the Bay of Fundy—some days feeling an increased motivation for recovery and then others feeling depleted of energy and strength. Some days you'll really want to beat this. Other times, "Eh... I don't really care right now."

LOW TIDE   HIGH TIDE

Maybe you've even had that experience since starting this program. It's OK. That's normal. It means you're human. Have you ever met anyone whose desires never fluctuate, never shift, and never waver? Neither have we. But let us know if you do, because we want their autograph!

It's common during the recovery process to experience conflicting desires. Plain and simple, our desires are not always fixed on the same goal or at the same level of intensity. At any given moment, part of you may want recovery and part of you may not. Because of this, we can end up profoundly inconsistent in our behavior. When the desire to work toward freedom is there, we are strong. When it's not, we can easily fall apart. At times, this results in a full-fledged war raging inside us—from "I really, really, really want to leave this behind!" to "I don't care anymore," to "I kind of, sort of want to end this addiction."

And let's be honest—sometimes your desire is to view pornography, right? Let's talk about that: how do you run from something that a part of you enjoys? Watching porn, after all, is not like hacking your arm off. There is a buzz to it—it feels good at first. But here you are reading *Fortify*, trying to back away from it. Why? Why walk away from something that can feel good? And how can you stay committed when part of you doesn't feel motivated? It's also easy to wonder whether your desires will be conflicting like this for the rest of your life.

Those are some tough questions—questions you'll have to answer for yourself. If you want our two cents, here it is:

First, this conflict of desires is a serious reminder of the importance of all the things we've discussed so far—including and especially securing your home base and getting others involved who can provide some accountability. If you don't involve other people and set up your environment to support your recovery, every time your desire shifts, you're likely to fall. As you give your brain and body what they need to detox and align with your true desires, of course, your need for external filtering and accountability can decrease. But for now, these parts of your Battle Strategy will be crucial protections for times when your desire is low. And over time, guess what: that deeper change can happen! The conflict in desires doesn't need to last forever!

There is a Cherokee legend of a grandfather's advice to a boy who was struggling. According to the story, the grandfather said, "Inside every human being, a constant battle rages—a battle between two wolves. One is evil—he is full of hate, lust, greed, and arrogance. The other wolf is good—full of love, compassion, honesty, and humility. These two wolves are constantly at war—both trying to dominate the individual."

The grandson thought about that for a minute and then asked, "Which wolf will win?" The old Cherokee simply replied, "Whichever one you feed."

How often do we fall victim to the two wolves—torn back and forth by competing feelings? Again, it's normal to have those competing desires, but what matters is which one you give more attention to. Each time you feed a desire it becomes stronger. So as you continuously feed the right desire—the desire pushing you toward recovery—eventually all other competing desires will starve.

So which desire are you feeding?

To help you maintain a strong desire for recovery, keep

your focus on ideas, messages, and activities that promote your desire for freedom. Do everything you can to surround yourself with things and people that will help you.

No matter how intense the ebb and flow of your own desire can get, you are still in the driver's seat. This doesn't mean that you won't have challenging days ahead. But when you do, you'll know how to get through them.

LEARNING FROM LOST BATTLES

Let's take a second to look at a reality of war. Nearly every victory experiences at least some casualties. Even with your best efforts, you will most likely not be perfect, especially in the beginning. In a weak moment, you may fall.

Too bad—you blew it. So much for freedom and recovery, right?

Of course not! Let's be real: relapse or setbacks are a common occurrence on the road to recovery. It's true that these falls can be serious. Like weeds, they threaten to choke off other progress you make. But at the same time, setbacks happen for all of us. The important thing is that you keep moving forward and not lose focus on the end goal.

In the moment of a setback, however, you will probably feel an intense pull to do the reverse—to continue falling deeper and deeper into the addiction cycle. Many of us get so discouraged that we think, "I blew it! So much for all that progress. What a waste!" And so one slip-up turns into several days of binging. And that's when we start to get to a dangerous spot. When one setback turns into binging, it really does threaten to reverse your progress.

So here's a tip: when a setback happens, stay away from both beating yourself up and from pretending it's not a big deal. Neither are healthy approaches. Instead, consider a more balanced approach in the aftermath of a setback that avoids both extremes.

Try rewinding the entire experience to watch carefully what happened in slow-motion, and then learn from it. What little choices led you to move toward using or starting the ritual? As you explore this, try tracing out the pattern, like backtracking through a lost battle's site. When you've got that image in mind, look for how you can set things up differently in the future, in preparation for when the next urge hits.

As you learn from your experiences, other powerful, even life-changing insights can arise. For instance, every slipup can remind you of a need for help and that you can't do this alone.

Also, pay attention to the way you feel in that moment after using. Many report feeling numb, empty, guilty, embarrassed, depressed, or even angry. While these emotions can lead someone to throw in the towel and spiral downward again, they can also lead the person to recommit and feel a determination to be stronger, saying, "I do not want to go through this again!"

Don't be too hard on yourself, though. Remember that you're not perfect and setbacks are common during a serious recovery. Rather than surrendering and giving up because of a failed moment, get back up and learn from the experience. Recommit again—not dramatically, but with quiet, humble desire. As author Mary Anne Radmacher said, "Sometimes courage is just saying, 'I will try again tomorrow.' And sometimes a hero is someone who just keeps going."

Take one day at a time, enjoying each 24 hours of freedom from pornography.

One more thing: when a setback occurs, it is easy to focus on how many times you've fallen. We can be so focused on our failed moments that we're not paying attention to the good moments—the ones that aren't failures. What if instead of thinking only of failed attempts, you focused on how many times you've gotten up, how many times you've turned away, how many times you've kept trying and the fact that you are trying at all!

Even when you've messed up, in that very next moment you can recalibrate. In the very next moment you can choose something that will strengthen you to go in another direction.

The very next moment can be very, very different.

BATTLE STRATEGY #17:

Create a plan for when a setback occurs. How are you going to respond so that you keep moving forward and maintain positive momentum?

(Go to your Battle Strategy in the back of the book on page 236 to answer.)

 **ACTION**

Read the poem below by Dr. D. H. Groberg.

"The Race"

Whenever I start to hang my head in front of failure's face, my downward fall is broken by the memory of a race. A children's race, young boys, young men; how I remember well, excitement sure, but also fear, it wasn't hard to tell.

They all lined up so full of hope, each thought to win that race or tie for first, or if not that, at least take second place. Their parents watched from off the side, each cheering for their son, and each boy hoped to show his folks that he would be the one.

The whistle blew and off they flew, like chariots of fire, to win, to be the hero there, was each young boy's desire. One boy in particular, whose dad was in the crowd, was running in the lead and thought, "My dad will be so proud."

But as he speeded down the field and crossed a shallow dip, the little boy who thought he'd win, lost his step and slipped. Trying hard to catch himself, his arms flew everyplace, and midst the laughter of the crowd he fell flat on his face.

As he fell, his hope fell too; he couldn't win it now. Humiliated, he just wished to disappear somehow. But as he fell his dad stood up and showed his anxious face, which to the boy so clearly said, "Get up and win that race!"

He quickly rose, no damage done, behind a bit that's all, and ran with all his mind and might to make up for his fall. So anxious to restore himself, to catch up and to win, his mind went faster than his legs. He slipped and fell again. He wished that he had quit before with only one disgrace. "I'm hopeless as a runner now, I shouldn't try to race." But through the laughing crowd he searched and found his father's face with a steady look that said again, "Get up and win that race!"

So he jumped up to try again, ten yards behind the last. "If I'm to gain those yards," he thought, "I've got to run real fast!" Exceeding everything he had, he regained eight, then ten... but trying hard to catch the lead, he slipped and fell again.

Defeat! He lay there silently. A tear dropped from his eye. "There's no sense running anymore! Three strikes I'm out! Why try? I've lost, so what's the use?" he thought. "I'll live with my disgrace." But then he thought about his dad, who soon he'd have to face.

"Get up," an echo sounded low, "you haven't lost at all, for all you have to do to win is rise each time you fall. Get up!" the echo urged him on, "Get up and take your place! You were not meant for failure here! Get up and win that race!"

So, up he rose to run once more, refusing to forfeit, and he resolved that win or lose, at least he wouldn't quit. So far behind the others now, the most he'd ever been, still he gave it all he had and ran like he could win.

Three times he'd fallen stumbling, three times he rose again. Too far behind to hope to win, he still ran to the end. They cheered another boy who crossed the line and won first place, head high and proud and happy—no falling, no disgrace.

But, when the fallen youngster crossed the line, in last place, the crowd gave him a greater cheer for finishing the race. And even though he came in last with head bowed low, unproud, you would have thought he'd won the race, to listen to the crowd.

And to his dad he sadly said, "I didn't do so well." "To me, you won," his father said. "You rose each time you fell." And now when things seem dark and bleak and difficult to face, the memory of that little boy helps me in my own race.

For all of life is like that race, with ups and downs and all. And all you have to do to win is rise each time you fall. And when depression and despair shout loudly in my face, another voice within me says, "Get up and win that race!"

CHECK-IN

Before we move on to the last chapter in the book, we wanted to quickly check in with you to see what you thought about some of the previous chapters: Fortify Yourself, Fortify Your Relationships, and Fortify Your World—or as we like to call it: Fortifying Your Life. Are you constantly working on replacing the dark portions of your life with light? Are you building healthy habits that can eventually strangle addiction's power over you?

Let's get specific about one particular section you read in Fortify Your Relationships: Time to Get Serious. Remember what this section was talking about? Accountability.

We weren't kidding when we said that getting a trusted adult involved is one of the most powerful and crucial steps in recovery. For something as serious as this fight, you need support—an individual or a group of individuals who are just as dedicated to your recovery as you are. Embrace the fact that there are individuals out there who want to help and want you to succeed.

For those of you who already have your accountability partner involved in your recovery, you know just how important they are. You probably noticed a feeling of relief when you finally opened up, as if you were able to share some of the weight of the addiction that you've been carrying around all by yourself.

How often are you checking in with your accountability partner? Do you need to bring others on to your support team? Did you decide to install accountability software onto your Internet-enabled devices to help keep you committed?

We want you to know that we are very proud of you for getting this far in the *Fortify* program. At this point you've probably made some great changes in your life that are making you stronger each day. You're getting better at S.T.A.R. and becoming more confident in your ability to beat your addiction. These are all great things that will continue to help push you toward recovery. However, you need to know that without an accountability partner, your chances of true recovery are limited. The likelihood of you falling back into your addiction after months and possibly even years of freedom is too great to risk by not involving someone else in your recovery process.

You may be holding back on getting an accountability partner because of embarrassment or feeling uncomfortable with the idea of talking to someone about this. But there are many people out there who can help you. If you don't want to talk to your family or friends, the counselor at your school is a great resource. They've most likely heard it before. And really, this is what they do for work—help people like you with concerns like this. They will help you stay committed, focused, and grounded. Without the help of an accountability partner, it's more likely that you'll have setbacks or even give up. Don't risk it. Remember, recovery is a process and having someone encourage you through the ups and downs makes all the difference.

Do it. You won't regret it.

CHAPTER EIGHT

BECOMING A FIGHTER

LOOKING BACK AND GETTING READY TO BEGIN

Well, that's it! You've reached the end of our program. If it feels like something is over, then think twice: you're just getting started! The real adventure is what happens from here on out.

As you know, our goal in *Fortify* is not to rehabilitate a bunch of sorry people. Rather, it's to equip, arm, and unleash an army of courageous Fighters to secure their own freedom and then to do some good in this world.

"Wait a minute," you're probably thinking. "If the point was never to gain total freedom by the end of this book, then why did I do this? What's the purpose of all this?"

The purpose and aim of *Fortify* has been to get you started on a path that will get you where you want to go.

Let's review how far we've come:

First, we explored some of the new discoveries about the brain's changeability and began to consider a new way to fight that went beyond the Incredible Hulk just-try-harder approach.

Second, we learned some hard truths about the enemy and gained a better understanding of how we can step out of the addiction cycle and move toward freedom.

Third, we learned some strategies that can help in the moments when an urge hits, as well as help prevent future battles from even happening.

Fourth, we dug deeper and explored how we can fortify ourselves, understanding that recovery is about far more than just resisting pornography. We spent some time reviewing each of our own unique strengths and vulnerabilities and how we can set ourselves up for a porn-free lifestyle.

Fifth, we took a hard look at our relationships and how to improve them—exploring ways to develop real relationships and avoid spending too much time on hollow ones. We also discussed how important getting a trusted adult involved is to your recovery.

Sixth, we looked at our mental diet and overall productivity. We learned that we can avoid many of the things we sometimes bring into our lives that may be setting us up for addiction.

Seventh, we faced head-on some counter attacks—ideas, messages, and challenges that will try to stunt your progress. This future, as we've discussed, will depend on your willingness to rise again—and again and again; to not stay down—to get up and keep at it.

In this final chapter, we're going to discuss a few other support options for moving forward—staying involved, giving back, and continuing to move in the right direction.

As we move forward, don't expect it will all be kittens, rainbows, and skipping through golden wheat fields (although that is a pretty sweet visual!) The truth is, it will probably be the opposite of that. If your experience is anything like others', this will take everything you've got—and more. It will probably be hard and may even kick your butt at times—but not forever!

Your freedom will depend in large part on your courage to respond bravely, your willingness to reach out for help, your dedication to practice, and your desire to reclaim your life. Even then, you will probably also need support from others to become free for good.

In a way, we have declared war on pornography. Rather than a war of aggression, however, ours is a battle to protect lives worth living, and families that deserve more than just barely surviving.

FAST FORWARD TO THE FUTURE

It can be motivating to fast-forward your life for a moment to think about a day when you're more serious about a romantic relationship in your own life. Imagine the conversation: you are sitting next to someone you care about to talk about the possibility of a life together. This person asks, "Is there anything else we need to talk about before we go for this and commit for good? After all, we need to be completely open before we make a big decision like this."

Scenario 1. You respond: "I used to struggle intensely with an addiction to pornography. It took everything I had, but eventually, over a period of time, I got free and have been that way for three years now. I'm stronger and better for having won that fight."

Scenario 2. You respond: "I currently struggle intensely with an addiction to pornography. I've tried but haven't been able to shake it. It's been nine years since I started struggling. It's still pretty tough."

It's a no-brainer which scenario any one of us would prefer. The question is, which trajectory are you going to follow?

Some people might believe that they can have a good, healthy relationship while still struggling with an addiction to pornography. While it's true that active addicts can still have some kind of romantic relationship, let's be honest about the limits. After many years of pornography addiction, it can actually become hard to feel true love for other people.

So while you may want to commit to someone else in the middle of an active addiction, you will probably struggle to have any desire to give what that person really needs — especially over the long-term. In other words, even if you feel the desire to commit to someone, what kind of relationship will it really be? How long will it really last? Problems with relationships are not always obvious. And real relationships—the lasting, enjoyable kind—require an ability to pay careful and continual attention to the emotional needs of another person. If your emotional apparatus has been trained for years by pornography to focus only on your own needs and desires, how is that supposed to happen?

And sexual relationships—the lasting, meaningful kind— require an ability to pay attention to the sexual needs of another person. But once again, if your sexual desires have been trained and distorted by years of pornography use to focus only on your own sexual cravings, how is that supposed to happen?

The answer to both questions is: it simply doesn't. Pornography addiction and healthy, lasting, loving relationships are mortal enemies. They just can't coexist.

Want a healthy, lasting romance? Make sure your heart and mind are free to love. And if they're not free now? Remember: the choice of which direction to go is yours. To quote C. S. Lewis, "Every time you make a choice, you are turning the core, central part of you into something a little different from what it was before. All of our lives, across many choices, we are slowly turning this central thing into one kind of a person or another" (Lewis, 1960). That's good news, right? At each moment we are all progressing toward one state or another.

Either you are moving toward living in harmony with yourself and others, and being free to do what you want, or you are moving toward a life centered on your own wants and being driven to satisfy them.

And when you finally do become free, don't think you have to live your life constantly on the verge of falling back into this addiction. As you leave this thing behind for good, you can become a powerful force for good in the lives of your family and friends—not in spite of all that has happened, but because of it.

We see you in this future day not vulnerable but full of strength and wisdom because of what you have learned.

In that day, you may realize that our greatest problem can turn out to be our most powerful teacher.

GET INVOLVED AND GIVE BACK

With your journey just beginning, we encourage you to come back often and refresh your memory on anything from different strategies to ways you can fortify deeper aspects of your life and prepare yourself for counter attacks.

Feel free to return to this program as often as you want during the recovery process. Each time you revisit a topic you'll learn new things—finding messages that you missed the first time around.

But we aren't raising an army of dedicated Fighters simply to help improve the lives of those inside this *Fortify* bubble. We're hoping to impact the larger world as well—one Fighter at a time. We need your help to spread this message, the message that pornography isn't cool, it's not healthy, and it hurts relationships.

After finishing this book, you're already more informed on this subject than the vast majority of people. It's up to us to help others understand just how harmful pornography can be and what recovery can look like. To help you do that, we invite you to join the Fight the New Drug movement by checking out our website and finding ways to get involved. The power of one passionate individual helping to educate their campus or community on the harmful effects of pornography using science, facts, and personal accounts can help others avoid its pitfalls. Go to www.fightthenewdrug.org to learn more.

Share informative blog posts and videos on your Facebook or Twitter pages. Or simply look for appropriate ways to have an open discussion about the subject among friends and family.

Whether you get involved with the Fight the New Drug movement or some other group with a similar mission, the point is to join something that allows you to give back. By taking a physically active role in this fight you will notice a strength and determination come into your life that will surprise you. You don't need to be fully recovered to get involved in a movement. The simple act of helping others escape these same pitfalls and habits will further motivate you and accelerate your own healing process.

BATTLE STRATEGY #18:

In what ways are you going to give back?

(Go to your Battle Strategy in the back of the book on page 236 to answer.)

✪ ACTION

Join the Fight the New Drug movement and help spread the word
in your area. Go to www.fightthenewdrug.org to get involved.

HELP BEYOND THE FORTIFY PROGRAM

Throughout this book we have explored the knowledge
and tools necessary for a lasting recovery. If you implement everything we've talked about and keep working
toward a fortified life, you will start to see major changes,
not only with your pornography habit but also with
nearly every other aspect of your life. You'll start to feel
more confident, happy, and at peace. You up for that?

Many of you probably feel satisfied with what the *Fortify*
program has taught you and feel completely confident
in your ability to move forward with the help of your
accountability partner. That's awesome!

There are, however, many of you reading this that want
nothing more than to feel relief from this addiction, but
just don't feel capable of doing it without professional
help. That is OK. Many addictions require the assistance
of a professional therapist to fully reach recovery. Don't
be ashamed; be excited. Acknowledging that you need
this professional help is another huge step toward the
long-term goals you've set for yourself.

From the beginning, we've shared with you why it's
important to pull this addiction out of secrecy and open
up to someone—someone you trust and who is willing to
help you. If you've done this, you should have a trusted
adult involved by now—like a parent, school counselor,
or religious leader—eager to help you do whatever it
takes throughout this process. If you and your accountability partner decide that finding and possibly paying

for the services of a professional therapist will be important for your recovery, go for it!

Working with an accountability partner, decide together on a therapist or facility that best meets your needs. One small tip: make sure this therapist will respect your value system. Like friends at school, not all therapists understand the dangers of pornography yet. You don't want to waste time with a therapist who will take you around in more circles. Choose professional help that understands what you're going through and will only add to how far you've come with Fortify.

So here's the question: do you already have someone involved that can help you? If not, let us recommend once again that you think about someone you trust and can see yourself approaching. It's so worth it. Compare for a minute the small discomfort of asking for help to the grandeur of recovery. What is your choice?

At this point, what really matters is getting the necessary help you need to rid your life of this addiction. Take what you've learned here in this book and let's rock and roll! Whatever it takes, let's do this!

BECOMING A FIGHTER

All right, this all sounds nice and good, maybe even something you are excited to pursue. In the meantime, today may still be hard for you. Maybe you're still struggling just to have one porn-free day. None of what we're describing will be quick, easy, or done by tomorrow. In the process of moving toward your freedom you will experience ups and downs that can get discouraging, to say the least.

Whatever else you think about yourself, your life, and your future—you've already proven one thing simply by participating in this program: you're a Fighter.

During World War II, when a Nazi assault threatened Great Britain, Prime Minister Winston Churchill said: "Never give in. Never give in. Never, never, never, never—in nothing, great or small, large or petty—never give in, except to convictions of honor and good sense. Never yield to force. Never yield to the apparently over-whelming might of the enemy ... Those who succeed keep getting up."

You may get to a point where you say, "I wish none of this had happened."

Anyone in your shoes will likely feel something like that. But this isn't something you can rewind. It has happened. All we have to decide is what to do with this moment, then the next one, then the next.

That is your test. The only tragedy for you would be giving up. As you walk down this path, have hope. Don't fear. This will take time, but it won't take forever. As we've discussed throughout, it will take everything you've got—and even that won't be enough in most cases. You'll also need help from others. We're here for you too—your Fighter brothers and sisters. All around you, an army of Fighters is being mobilized. Equipped and determined, we are moving in the same direction. And we will not be stopped. To finish, sign the Fighter Pledge:

THE FIGHTER PLEDGE

Now is the time for me to stand and help others overcome that which has affected my family, my friends, and my community. I will avoid exposure to this powerful drug called pornography. I will be a source of strength to those who need support and accept help when I am in need. I will be a voice of reason among the clatter of self-serving opinion. Too many have suffered. Too many have sacrificed. I must be open about a topic no one wants to discuss.

As a Fighter...

I AM STRONG

I have joined an army of support-
ers and will rely on their strength
as well as my own to help others
understand how pornography is
affecting their lives.

I AM BOLD

*I am not afraid to speak openly
about the effects of pornography.*

I AM UNDERSTANDING

I am aware of the difficulty some may face in ridding their lives of pornography. Rather than condemning actions, I will help relieve their shame.

I AM ACCEPTING

*I know that judging others'
actions is not my place. I will
respectfully promote my opin-
ions but in the end, allow
others to choose for themselves
what course they will take.*

I AM SEXY

There is nothing more sexy than two committed individuals together. I will not be that lone ranger looking for love from behind the computer screen.

I AM OPEN-MINDED

I recognize that mine is not the only opinion. I will respect others' points of view just as I expect them to do the same for me.

I AM ENCOURAGING

I will not turn my back on those that need my help. I will commit to helping them overcome the effects of pornography.

I AM REAL

I do not pursue false imitations or masked presentations. I am confident enough in myself to be genuine.

I AM A TRUE LOVER

*I seek real relationships and
shun their hollow counterfeits.*

I AM A REBEL

I refuse to follow the status quo. I will do what needs to be done and say what needs to be said, regardless of what is popular, in order to help foster change.

I AM A FIGHTER.

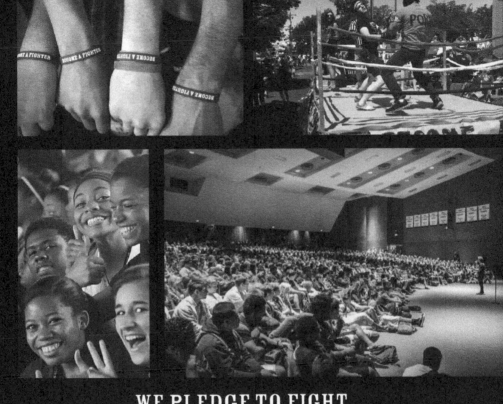

WE PLEDGE TO FIGHT.
DO YOU?

X_____

*Go online to www.FightTheNewDrug.org and sign the
Fighter Pledge to join a global army of fighters!*

Follow us online!

BATTLE TRACKER

WHEN YOU CAN ACTU-ALLY SEE AND RECORD YOUR DAY-TO-DAY BATTLES AND TRACK YOUR SUCCESSES AND SETBACKS, YOU CAN GAIN AN UNDER-STANDING THAT WILL GIVE CLARITY AND STRENGTH TO YOUR FIGHT AGAINST POR-NOGRAPHY.

To help you accomplish this we're giving you your very own Battle Tracker, which is essentially a calendar to track your battles and your victories. You'll notice that each day has three separate columns that represent morning, day, and night (☼ ☀ ☾). In each column there are four different boxes with a numerical value ranging from 0 to 3. Each number represents the intensity of a particular urge or what we like to call a battle.

FOR EXAMPLE, if a strong urge to view pornography hits you in the morning then you'd put an X in the very top box in the "morning" column. If you had no urge to view pornography in the afternoon then you'd put an X in very bottom box in the "day" column, indicating that you had no battle during that time of day.

GIVING EACH BATTLE A RATING IS IMPORTANT. At first you may stumble

with a level 1 battle but over time, as you get stronger, you may get to the point where you experience two separate level 3 battles in a single day without having a setback. Each victory you experience will make you stronger for the next battle.

YOU'LL ALSO NOTICE A PLACE TO MARK WHETHER OR NOT YOU HAD A SETBACK THAT DAY. It's never easy to admit temporary

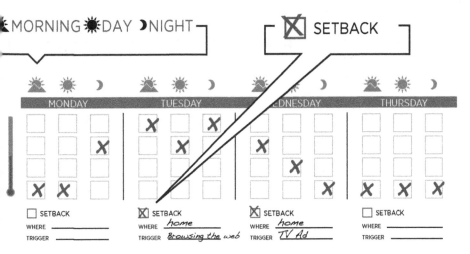

☀MORNING ☀DAY ❯NIGHT

☒ SETBACK

	MONDAY			TUESDAY			WEDNESDAY			THURSDAY	
			X		X						
	X			X		X					
							X				
X	X							X	X	X	X

☐ SETBACK	☒ SETBACK	☒ SETBACK	☐ SETBACK
WHERE ____	WHERE _home_	WHERE _home_	WHERE ____
TRIGGER ____	TRIGGER _Browsing the web_	TRIGGER _TV Ad_	TRIGGER ____

INTENSITY OF URGE

defeat, but it is important that you do. Some of our Fighters mark this box with a red X. The fewer X's they see in a given month, the better. During your first few months you may experience several more defeats than you had hoped. However, those who stick to it and keep using their Battle Tracker can see their progress over time.

BELOW THE CHART YOU CAN SPECIFY WHERE THE SETBACK OCCURRED AND WHAT TRIGGERED THAT PARTICULAR BATTLE (TV, browsing the web, a billboard, etc). This will help you recognize patterns and give you the necessary information to make adjustments and gain an advantage over your addiction.

Using the Weekly, Monthly, and Quarterly Reports

In order to make a clean recovery from pornography addiction, it is vital that you track your progress. Just as important as tracking your progress, however, is understanding what the data means and then using it to improve.

We've included **weekly, monthly, and quarterly (3 months) reports** for doing just that. At the end of each week, tally up your weekly scores and report them on the weekly report page. Do the same for the end of each month and quarter. On the monthly and quarterly reports, divide the number of victories (days without a setback) by the total number of days. This will give you your **Victory Rate**.

As you improve and begin to live a pornography-free life, this victory rate should increase! Strive for zero-tolerance. We understand that this is hard, but we know that with time you, just like many others, can eventually reach a **100% Victory Rate!**

MONTHLY REPORT

MONTHLY TOTALS

HOW MANY VICTORIES?	25
HOW MANY SETBACKS?	5
OVERALL STRONGEST TRIGGER?	youtube
WHERE WERE YOU MOST VULNERABLE	Bedroom
WHAT TIME OF DAY IS THE HARDEST?	Night

PROGRESS REPORT

TOTAL NUMBER OF VICTORIES:	25
TOTAL NUMBER OF DAYS:	30

NOW DIVIDE THE NUMBER OF DAYS BY THE NUMBER OF VICTORIES TO FIND OUT YOUR VICTORY RATE.

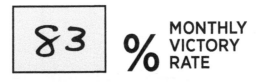

83 **%** **MONTHLY VICTORY RATE**

BATTLE TRACKER

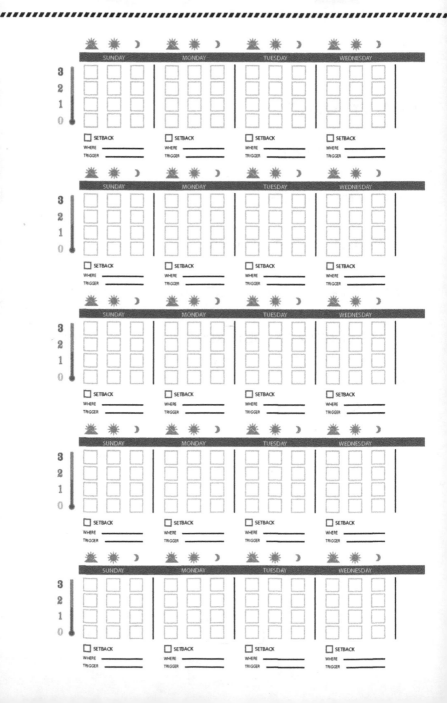

	SUNDAY	MONDAY	TUESDAY	WEDNESDAY
3 2 1 0	☐ SETBACK	☐ SETBACK	☐ SETBACK	☐ SETBACK
	WHERE _____ TRIGGER _____	WHERE _____ TRIGGER _____	WHERE _____ TRIGGER _____	WHERE _____ TRIGGER _____

	SUNDAY	MONDAY	TUESDAY	WEDNESDAY
3 2 1 0	☐ SETBACK	☐ SETBACK	☐ SETBACK	☐ SETBACK
	WHERE _____ TRIGGER _____	WHERE _____ TRIGGER _____	WHERE _____ TRIGGER _____	WHERE _____ TRIGGER _____

	SUNDAY	MONDAY	TUESDAY	WEDNESDAY
3 2 1 0	☐ SETBACK	☐ SETBACK	☐ SETBACK	☐ SETBACK
	WHERE _____ TRIGGER _____	WHERE _____ TRIGGER _____	WHERE _____ TRIGGER _____	WHERE _____ TRIGGER _____

	SUNDAY	MONDAY	TUESDAY	WEDNESDAY
3 2 1 0	☐ SETBACK	☐ SETBACK	☐ SETBACK	☐ SETBACK
	WHERE _____ TRIGGER _____	WHERE _____ TRIGGER _____	WHERE _____ TRIGGER _____	WHERE _____ TRIGGER _____

	SUNDAY	MONDAY	TUESDAY	WEDNESDAY
3 2 1 0	☐ SETBACK	☐ SETBACK	☐ SETBACK	☐ SETBACK
	WHERE _____ TRIGGER _____	WHERE _____ TRIGGER _____	WHERE _____ TRIGGER _____	WHERE _____ TRIGGER _____

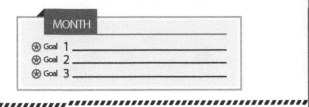

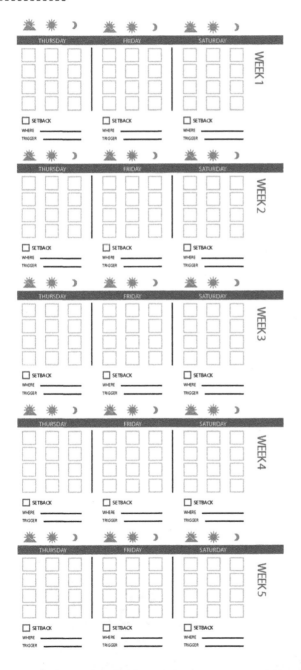

WEEK 1

THURSDAY | FRIDAY | SATURDAY

☐ SETBACK ☐ SETBACK ☐ SETBACK
WHERE _____ WHERE _____ WHERE _____
TRIGGER _____ TRIGGER _____ TRIGGER _____

WEEK 2

THURSDAY | FRIDAY | SATURDAY

☐ SETBACK ☐ SETBACK ☐ SETBACK
WHERE _____ WHERE _____ WHERE _____
TRIGGER _____ TRIGGER _____ TRIGGER _____

WEEK 3

THURSDAY | FRIDAY | SATURDAY

☐ SETBACK ☐ SETBACK ☐ SETBACK
WHERE _____ WHERE _____ WHERE _____
TRIGGER _____ TRIGGER _____ TRIGGER _____

WEEK 4

THURSDAY | FRIDAY | SATURDAY

☐ SETBACK ☐ SETBACK ☐ SETBACK
WHERE _____ WHERE _____ WHERE _____
TRIGGER _____ TRIGGER _____ TRIGGER _____

WEEK 5

THURSDAY | FRIDAY | SATURDAY

☐ SETBACK ☐ SETBACK ☐ SETBACK
WHERE _____ WHERE _____ WHERE _____
TRIGGER _____ TRIGGER _____ TRIGGER _____

MONTHLY REPORT

MONTHLY TOTALS

HOW MANY VICTORIES?	
HOW MANY SETBACKS?	
OVERALL STRONGEST TRIGGER?	
WHERE WERE YOU MOST VULNERABLE?	
WHAT TIME OF DAY IS THE HARDEST?	

PROGRESS REPORT

TOTAL NUMBER OF VICTORIES:

TOTAL NUMBER OF DAYS:

NOW DIVIDE THE NUMBER OF DAYS BY THE NUMBER OF VICTORIES TO FIND OUT YOUR VICTORY RATE.

 **% MONTHLY VICTORY RATE**

BATTLE TRACKER

	SUNDAY	MONDAY	TUESDAY	WEDNESDAY
3				
2				
1				
0				

SETBACK WHERE TRIGGER | SETBACK WHERE TRIGGER | SETBACK WHERE TRIGGER | SETBACK WHERE TRIGGER

	SUNDAY	MONDAY	TUESDAY	WEDNESDAY
3				
2				
1				
0				

SETBACK WHERE TRIGGER | SETBACK WHERE TRIGGER | SETBACK WHERE TRIGGER | SETBACK WHERE TRIGGER

	SUNDAY	MONDAY	TUESDAY	WEDNESDAY
3				
2				
1				
0				

SETBACK WHERE TRIGGER | SETBACK WHERE TRIGGER | SETBACK WHERE TRIGGER | SETBACK WHERE TRIGGER

	SUNDAY	MONDAY	TUESDAY	WEDNESDAY
3				
2				
1				
0				

SETBACK WHERE TRIGGER | SETBACK WHERE TRIGGER | SETBACK WHERE TRIGGER | SETBACK WHERE TRIGGER

	SUNDAY	MONDAY	TUESDAY	WEDNESDAY
3				
2				
1				
0				

SETBACK WHERE TRIGGER | SETBACK WHERE TRIGGER | SETBACK WHERE TRIGGER | SETBACK WHERE TRIGGER

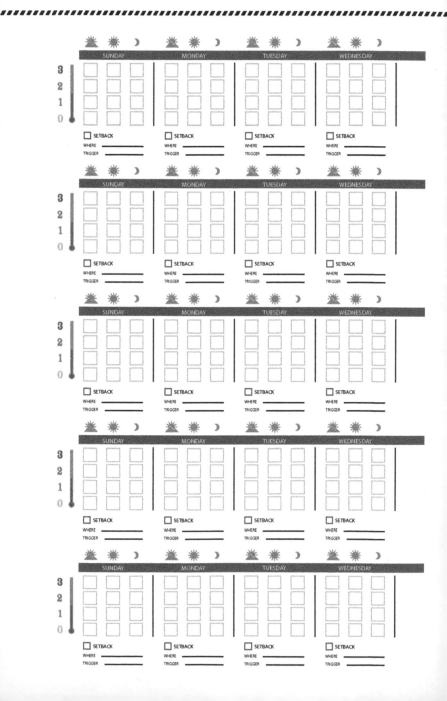

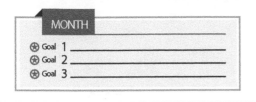

MONTH

⊕ Goal 1 _____
⊕ Goal 2 _____
⊕ Goal 3 _____

🌅 ☀ 🌙	🌅 ☀ 🌙	🌅 ☀ 🌙	
THURSDAY	FRIDAY	SATURDAY	WEEK 1

☐ SETBACK ☐ SETBACK ☐ SETBACK
WHERE _____ WHERE _____ WHERE _____
TRIGGER _____ TRIGGER _____ TRIGGER _____

🌅 ☀ 🌙	🌅 ☀ 🌙	🌅 ☀ 🌙	
THURSDAY	FRIDAY	SATURDAY	WEEK 2

☐ SETBACK ☐ SETBACK ☐ SETBACK
WHERE _____ WHERE _____ WHERE _____
TRIGGER _____ TRIGGER _____ TRIGGER _____

🌅 ☀ 🌙	🌅 ☀ 🌙	🌅 ☀ 🌙	
THURSDAY	FRIDAY	SATURDAY	WEEK 3

☐ SETBACK ☐ SETBACK ☐ SETBACK
WHERE _____ WHERE _____ WHERE _____
TRIGGER _____ TRIGGER _____ TRIGGER _____

🌅 ☀ 🌙	🌅 ☀ 🌙	🌅 ☀ 🌙	
THURSDAY	FRIDAY	SATURDAY	WEEK 4

☐ SETBACK ☐ SETBACK ☐ SETBACK
WHERE _____ WHERE _____ WHERE _____
TRIGGER _____ TRIGGER _____ TRIGGER _____

🌅 ☀ 🌙	🌅 ☀ 🌙	🌅 ☀ 🌙	
THURSDAY	FRIDAY	SATURDAY	WEEK 5

☐ SETBACK ☐ SETBACK ☐ SETBACK
WHERE _____ WHERE _____ WHERE _____
TRIGGER _____ TRIGGER _____ TRIGGER _____

MONTHLY REPORT

MONTHLY TOTALS

HOW MANY VICTORIES?	
HOW MANY SETBACKS?	
OVERALL STRONGEST TRIGGER?	
WHERE WERE YOU MOST VULNERABLE?	
WHAT TIME OF DAY IS THE HARDEST?	

PROGRESS REPORT

TOTAL NUMBER OF VICTORIES:

TOTAL NUMBER OF DAYS:

NOW DIVIDE THE NUMBER OF DAYS BY THE NUMBER OF VICTORIES
TO FIND OUT YOUR VICTORY RATE.

 **% MONTHLY VICTORY RATE**

BATTLE TRACKER

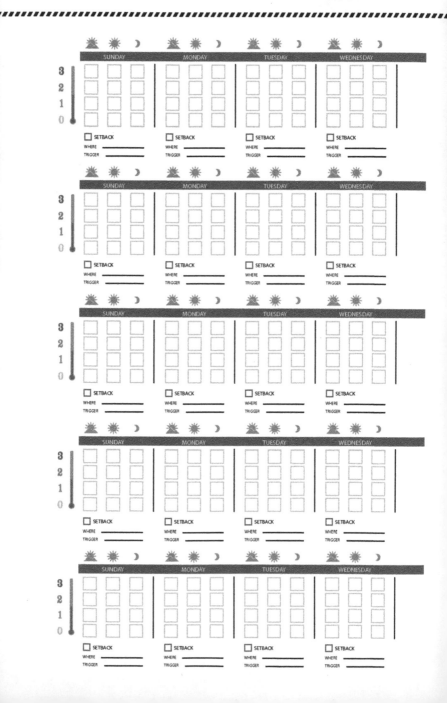

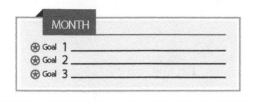

MONTH _____

- ⊛ Goal 1 _____
- ⊛ Goal 2 _____
- ⊛ Goal 3 _____

WEEK 1

THURSDAY | FRIDAY | SATURDAY

☐ SETBACK ☐ SETBACK ☐ SETBACK
WHERE ____ WHERE ____ WHERE ____
TRIGGER ____ TRIGGER ____ TRIGGER ____

WEEK 2

THURSDAY | FRIDAY | SATURDAY

☐ SETBACK ☐ SETBACK ☐ SETBACK
WHERE ____ WHERE ____ WHERE ____
TRIGGER ____ TRIGGER ____ TRIGGER ____

WEEK 3

THURSDAY | FRIDAY | SATURDAY

☐ SETBACK ☐ SETBACK ☐ SETBACK
WHERE ____ WHERE ____ WHERE ____
TRIGGER ____ TRIGGER ____ TRIGGER ____

WEEK 4

THURSDAY | FRIDAY | SATURDAY

☐ SETBACK ☐ SETBACK ☐ SETBACK
WHERE ____ WHERE ____ WHERE ____
TRIGGER ____ TRIGGER ____ TRIGGER ____

WEEK 5

THURSDAY | FRIDAY | SATURDAY

☐ SETBACK ☐ SETBACK ☐ SETBACK
WHERE ____ WHERE ____ WHERE ____
TRIGGER ____ TRIGGER ____ TRIGGER ____

MONTHLY REPORT

MONTHLY TOTALS

HOW MANY VICTORIES?	
HOW MANY SETBACKS?	
OVERALL STRONGEST TRIGGER?	
WHERE WERE YOU MOST VULNERABLE?	
WHAT TIME OF DAY IS THE HARDEST?	

PROGRESS REPORT

TOTAL NUMBER OF VICTORIES:

TOTAL NUMBER OF DAYS:

NOW DIVIDE THE NUMBER OF DAYS BY THE NUMBER OF VICTORIES TO FIND OUT YOUR VICTORY RATE.

% MONTHLY VICTORY RATE

BATTLE STRATEGY

BATTLE STRATEGY #1
Why are you here? What do you hope to gain or accomplish from this book? What do you want your recovery to look like one year from now?

_____

_____

_____

_____

_____

_____

_____

_____

_____

_____

BATTLE STRATEGY #2
Create your own list of passions or things that you absolutely love doing, so that you'll have plenty of options when the next urge hits. You can also write those passions down on a small piece of paper and carry the list with you in your pocket or wallet. Everybody is going to have different passions that work for them, so make it your own.

_____

_____

_____

_____

_____

_____

_____

_____

_____

BATTLE STRATEGY #3

How are you going to implement a zero-tolerance mindset in your life? What boundaries are you going to set for yourself?

_____

_____

_____

_____

_____

_____

_____

_____

_____

_____

BATTLE STRATEGY #4

What are you going to do to secure your home base? What are you going to surround yourself with? What are you going to get rid of? What are you going to allow into your life?

_____

_____

_____

_____

_____

_____

_____

_____

BATTLE STRATEGY #5
Write about the things in your life that you love or desire more than pornography. Try to think of at least one anchor for each category (people, passions, and purpose). Explain why each thing is more important than your addiction to pornography.

_____

_____

_____

_____

_____

_____

_____

_____

_____

_____

BATTLE STRATEGY #6
Write out a list of individuals that you could imagine being supportive of your desire to recover. This could include any family members, religious leaders, and other people you trust. Keep this list around as you think about having accountability partners.

_____

_____

_____

_____

_____

_____

_____

_____

_____

_____

BATTLE STRATEGY #7
If this area is relevant to you and you have not been able to
fully process some past experiences, find and talk to a trusted
adult. Who, specifically, can you talk to? When do you plan to
talk to them?

_____

_____

_____

_____

_____

_____

_____

_____

_____

_____

BATTLE STRATEGY #8
After taking a deeper look into the rest of your life, can you
identify any other areas that seem a little out of control? Write
them down and then brainstorm different ideas to help you
kick these other unwanted behaviors.

_____

_____

_____

_____

_____

_____

_____

_____

_____

_____

BATTLE STRATEGY #9
How would it feel to commit to being truly physically healthy?
No matter where you are with addiction, making this decision
would be one step closer to your freedom. What can you do to
increase your physical activity? What can you do to improve
your eating habits? What time are you going to go to bed and
what time are you going to wake up every day?

_____

_____

_____

_____

_____

_____

_____

_____

_____

_____

BATTLE STRATEGY #10
Make a list of three things that you are going to implement into
your life that will help build your sense of self-worth.

_____

_____

_____

_____

_____

_____

_____

_____

_____

BATTLE STRATEGY #11
List out some ideas of how you can increase the real connections in your life. Be specific.

_____

_____

_____

_____

_____

_____

_____

_____

_____

_____

BATTLE STRATEGY #12
Which relationships in your life are you going to focus on? What specific actions are you going to take to strengthen them?

_____

_____

_____

_____

_____

_____

_____

_____

_____

_____

_____

_____

_____

BATTLE STRATEGY #13
Refer back to the list of possible accountability partners you created earlier. Map out a plan to approach one of these individuals based on the tips given on page 131.

_____

_____

_____

_____

_____

_____

_____

_____

_____

_____

BATTLE STRATEGY #14
What actions are you going to take to improve your own mental diet? Be specific.

_____

_____

_____

_____

_____

_____

_____

_____

_____

_____

BATTLE STRATEGY #15
What changes are you going to make in your life to stay busy and be more productive?

_____

_____

_____

_____

_____

_____

_____

_____

_____

_____

BATTLE STRATEGY #16
List the three biggest stresses in your life right now and how you plan on responding to those stresses in a healthy way.

_____

_____

_____

_____

_____

_____

_____

_____

_____

_____

_____

_____

_____

_____

BATTLE STRATEGY #17
Create a plan for when a setback occurs. How are you going to respond so that you keep moving forward and maintain positive momentum?

_____

_____

_____

_____

_____

_____

_____

_____

_____

BATTLE STRATEGY #18
In what ways are you going to give back?

_____

_____

_____

_____

_____

_____

_____

_____

_____

_____

_____

BOOK REFERENCES

Anderson, G. (2010). "Loneliness Among Older Adults: A National Survey of Adults 45+." AARP Research Center: Surveys and Statistics. Retrieved from http://www.aarp.org/personal-growth/transitions/info09-2010/loneliness_2010.html

Anderson, K. (1992). "Pornography." Retrieved from http://www.leaderu.com/orgs/probe/docs/porno.html

Baer, J. (2012). "11 Shocking New Social Media Statistics in America." Convince and Convert: The Social Habit. Retrieved from http://www.convinceandconvert.com/the-social-habit/11-shocking-new-social-media-statistics-in-america/

Benjamin, B. (2000). "The Primacy of Human Touch." Health Touch News. Issue # 2. Retrieved from http://www.benbenjamin.net/pdfs/Issue2.pdf

Daines, M. and Shumway, T. (2012). "Pornography and Divorce.7th Annual Conference on Empirical Legal Studies Paper." California: Sanford Law School

Ettlinger, S. (2007). Twinkie, Deconstructed. New York: Hudson Street Press.

Frankyl, V. (2006). Man's Search For Meaning. Boston: Beacon Press

Ghilan, M. (2012). "How Watching Pornography Changes the Brain." Retrieved from http://www.suhaibwebb.com/ummah/men/how-watch--pornography-changes-the-brain/ Goodman, B. (Writer, Director & Producer) and Maggio J. (Director & Producer). (2008).

"Kinsey Establishes the Institute for Sex Research." American Experience: Kinsey. Saint Paul Minneapolis, MN: Twin Cities Public Television, Inc. and Ark Media for American Experience.

Hardoon, K. K., Gupta, R. and Deverensky, J.L. (2004). "Psychosocial variables associated with adolescent gambling." Psychology of Addictive Behaviors, 18, 170–179.

Kabat-Zinn, J. (2005). Full catastrophe living: Using the wisdom of your body and mind to face stress, pain and illness. The program of the stress reduction clinic at the University of Massachusetts Medical Center. Bantam Dell: New York.

Kerner, I. (2011). "How Porn Is Changing Our Sex Lives." CNN. Retrieved from http://thechart.blogs.cnn.com/2011/01/20/how-porn-is-changing-our-sex-lives/

Kinsey, A. C. and Martin, C. E. (1948). Sexual Behavior in the Human Male. Bloomington, IN: Indiana University Press. Pg: 178-180.

Klinenberg, E. (2010). Going Solo: The Extraordinary Rise and Surprising Appeal of Living Alone. New York: Penguin Group.

Krasnova, H., Wenninger, H., Widjaja, T. and Buxmann, P. (2013). "Envy on facebook: A hidden threat to users' life satisfaction?" Retrieved from http://warhol.wiwi.hu-berlin.de/~hkrasnova/Ongoing_Research_files/WI%202013%20Final%20Submission%20Krasnova.pdf

Lewis, C.S. Mere Christianity. New York: Macmillan, 1960.

Lubben, S. (2012). "Porn Stars To Testify Against Pornographer. Truth Behind the Fantasy of Porn." Retrieved at: http://www.shelleylubben.com/article_categories/Ex%20 Porn%20Star%20Stories

Manning, J. (2006). "The Impact of Internet Pornography on Marriage and the Family: A Review of the Research." Sexual Addiction and Compulsivity. Kentucky: Taylor & Francis Group,131-165

Marche, S. (2012). "Is Facebook Making Us Lonely?" The Atlantic. Retrieved from http://www.theatlantic.com/ magazine/archive/2012/05/is-facebook-making-us-lonely/308930/

Musil, S. (2012, May 20). Retrieved from http://news.cnet. com/8301-1023_3-57437973-93/schmidt-challenges-grads-to-turn-off-the-screen-for-an-hour-a-day/

National Sleep Foundation (2011). "Teens and Sleep." Retrieved from http://www.sleepfoundation.org/article/ sleep-topics/teens-and-sleep

Orbach, S. (2009). Bodies. New York: Picador.

Paul, P. (2005) Pornified: How Pornography is Transforming our Lives, our Relationships and our Families. New York: Times Books.

Peng, J. (2012). "Racy Scenes Encourage Greater Sexual Activity." U Wire: The College Network. Retrieved from http://uwire.com/2012/07/24/racy-scenes-encouragegreater-sexual-activity/

Putnam, R. (2000). Bowling Alone: The Collapse and Revival of American Community. New York: Simon and Schuster.

Reboot. (2010). Retrieved from http://www.sabbathmanifesto.org/unplug/

ScienceDaily (1998)."Carnegie Mellon Study Reveals Negative Potential of Heavy Internet Use on Emotional Well Being." Retrieved from http://www.sciencedaily.com/releases/1998/09/980901024936.htm

Schmidt, E. (2012). "Google Leader: Unplug and Reconnect." Unplug and Reconnect. Retrieved from http://unplugreconnect.com/articles/spreading-the-word/

Sivulka, Juliann (1997). Sex, Soap and Cigarettes. Belmont, CA: Wadsworth.

Stucker , V. (2013, February 21). Category archives: Virgil stucker. Retrieved from http://cooperriisblog.org/category/virgil-stucker/

Van Praag, H., Christie, B. R., Sejnowski, T.J. and Gage, F. (1999). "Running Enhances Neurogenesis, Learning, and Long-term Potentiation in Mice." Proceedings of the National Academy of the Sciences of the United States of America, Vol. 96(23), 13427-13431.

Zillmann D. and Bryant J. (1984). "Effects of massive exposure to pornography." In Malamuth, N.M. and Donnerstein, E. (Eds): Pornography and Sexual Aggression. New York: Academic Press.

Zimbardo, P. and Duncan, N. (2012). "The Demise of Guys." New York: TED Conferences, LLC.

FORTIFY INVENTORY REFERENCES

(Studies and Scholarship on which the Fortify Inventory Is Based)

Adams, K. M. and Robinson, D. W. (2001). "Shame reduction, affect regulation, and sexual boundary development: Essential building blocks of sexual addiction treatment." Sexual Addiction and Compulsivity, Vol. 8, 23-44.

Ahrold, T. K., Farmer, M., Trapnell, P. D. and Meston, C. M. (2010). "The relationship among sexual attitudes, sexual fantasy, and religiosity." Archives of Sexual Behavior, Vol. 40, 619-630.

Anderson, K. J. (2005). "Internet use among college students: an exploratory study." Journal of American College Health, Vol. 50(1):21–6.

Bakken, I. J., Wenzel, H. G., Götestam, K. G., Johansson, A. and Oren, A. (2009). "Internet addiction among Norwegian adults: a stratified probability sample study." Scandinavian Journal of Psychology, Vol. 50(2):121–7.

Baltazar, A., Helm, H. W., McBride, D., Hopkins, G. and Stevens, J. V. (2010). "Internet pornography use in the context of external and internal religisoity." Journal of Psychology and Theology, Vol. 38(1), 32–40.

Batthyány, D., Müller, K. W., Benker, F. and Wölfling, K. (2009). "Computer game playing: clinical characteristics of dependence and abuse among adolescents." Wien

Klin Wochenschr, Vol. 121(15–16):502–9.

"Behavioural addictions: Common features and treatment implications." British Journal of Addiction, Vol. 85(11), 1417–1419.

Berlin, F. S. (2008). "Basic science and neurobiological research: Potential relevance to sexual compulsivity." Psychiatric Clinics of North America, Vol. 31(4), 623–642.

Beutel, M. E., Brähler, E., Glaesmer, H., Kuss, D. J., Wölfling, K. and Müller, K. W. (2011). "Regular and problematic leisure-time Internet use in the community: results from a German population-based survey."

Bradley, B. (1990). Cyberpsychology, Behavior & Social Networks, Vol. 14(5):291–6.

Bryant, J. and Rockwell, S. C. (1994). "Effects of massive exposure to sexually oriented prime-time television programming on adolescents' moral judgment." In D. Zillmann, Bryant, J. and Huston, A. (Eds.), Media, children, and the family: Social scientific, psychodynamic, and clinical perspectives. Hillsdale: N.J. Lawrence Erlbaum Associates, Inc.

Cameron, K. A., Salazar, L. F., Bernhardt, J. M., Burgess-Whitman, N., Wingood, G. M. and DiClemente, R. J. (2005). "Adolescents' experience with sex on the Web: Results from online focus groups." Journal of Adolescence, Vol. 28(4), 535–540.

Caplan, S. E. (2005). "A social skill account of problematic Internet use." Journal of Communication, Vol. 55, 721–736.

Caplan, S. E. (2007). "Relations among loneliness, social anxiety, and problematic internet use." Cyberpsychology & Behavior, Vol. 10(2):234–42.

Ceyhan, A. A. (2008). "Predictors of problematic Internet use on Turkish university students." Cyberpsychology & Behavior, Vol. 11(3):363–6.

Chak K. and Leung, L. (2004). "Shyness and locus of control as predictors of internet addiction and internet use." Cyberpsychology & Behavior, Vol. 7(5):559–70.

Choi, K., Son, H., Park, M., Han, J., Kim, K., Lee, B. and Gwak, H. (2009). "Internet overuse and excessive daytime sleepiness in adolescents." Psychiatry & Clinical Neurosciences, Vol. 63(4):455–62.

Chou, C., Sinha, A. P. and Zhao, H. (2010). "Commercial Internet filters: Perils and opportunities." Decision Support Systems, Vol. 48(4), 521–530.

Corona, G., Ricca, V., Boddi, V., Bandini, E., Lotti, F., Fisher, A. D., Sforza, A., Forti, G., Mannucci, E. and Maggi, M. (2010). "Autoeroticism, mental health, and organic disturbances in patients with erectile dysfunction." The Journal of Sexual Medicine, Vol. 7(1), 182–191.

Deng, Y. X., Hu, M., Hu, G. Q., Wang, L. S. and Sun, Z. Q. (2007). "An investigation on the prevalence of internet addiction disorder in middle school students of Hunan province." Zhonghua Liu Xing Bing Xue Za Zhi, Vol. 28(5), 445-448.

Dong, G., Lu, Q., Zhou, H. and Zhao, X. (2011). "Precursor or sequela: pathological disorders in people with Internet addiction disorder." PLoS One, Vol. 6(2):E14703.

Dowell, E. B., Burgess, A. W. and Cavanaugh, D. J. (2009). "Clustering of internet risk behaviors in a middle school student population." Journal of School Health, Vol. 79(11), 547–553.

Echeburúa, E. and De Corral, P. (2010). "Addiction to new technologies and to online social networking in young people: A new challenge." Adicciones, Vol. 22(2):91–5.

Ferraro, G., Caci, B., D'Amico, A. and Di Blasi, M. (2007). "Internet addiction disorder: an Italian study." Cyberpsychology & Behavior, Vol. 10(2):170–5.

Gao, Y., Li, L. P., Kim, J. H., Congdon, N., Lau, J. and Griffiths, S. (2010). "The impact of parental migration on health status and health behaviours among left behind adolescent school children in China." BMC Public Health, Vol. 10:56.

Gardos, P. S. and Mosher, D. L. (1999). "Gender differences in reactions to viewing pornography vignettes: Essential or interpretive?" Journal of Psychology and Human Sexuality, Vol. 11, 65–83.

Gentile, D. A., Choo, H., Liau, A., Sim, T., Li, D., Fung, D. and Khoo, A. (2011). "Pathological video game use among youths: A two-year longitudinal study." Pediatrics, Vol. 127(2):e319–29.

Grüsser, S. M., Thalemann, R., Albrecht, U. and Thalemann, C. N. (2005). "Excessive computer usage in adolescents — results of a psychometric evaluation." Wien Klin Wochenschr, Vol. 117(5–6):188–95.

Henry, J. (2002). "See No Evil: How Internet filters affect the search for online health information." Washington: The Henry J. Kaiser Family Foundation.

Hill, A., Briken, P. and Berner, W. (2007). "Pornography and sexual abuse in the Internet." Bundesgesundheitsblatt Gesundheitsforschung Gesundheitsschutz, Vol. 50(1):90– 102.

Jang, K. S., Hwang, S. Y. and Choi, J. Y. (2008). "Internet addiction and psychiatric symptoms among Korean adolescents." Journal of School Health, Vol. 78(3):165–71.

June, K. J., Sohn, S. Y., So, A. Y., Yi, G. M. and Park, S. H. (2007). "A study of factors that influence Internet addiction, smoking, and drinking in high school students". Taehan Kanho Hakhoe Chi, Vol. 37(6):872–82.

Ko, C. H., Hsiao, S., Liu, G. C., Yen, J. Y., Yang, M. J. and Yen, C. F. (2010). "The characteristics of decision making, potential to take risks, and personality of college students with Internet addiction." Psychiatry Research, Vol. 175(1–2):121–5.

Ko, C. H., Yen, J. Y., Chen, C. C., Chen, S. H. and Yen, C. F. (2005). "Gender differences and related factors affecting online gaming addiction among Taiwanese adolescents." Journal of Nervous and Mental Disease, Vol. 193(4):273–7.

Ko, C.H., Yen, J. Y., Liu, S. C., Huang, C. F. and Yen, C. F. (2009). "The associations between aggressive behaviors and Internet addiction and online activities in adolescents." Journal of Adolescence Health, Vol. 44(6):598–605.

Korkeila, J., Kaarlas, S., Jääskeläinen, M., Vahlberg, T. and Taiminen, T. (2010). "Attached to the web: Harmful use of the Internet and its correlates." European Psychiatry, Vol. 25(4):236–41.

Kuhn, C., Johnson, M., Thomae, A., Luo, B., Simon, S. A., Zhou, G. and Walker, Q. D. (2010). "The emergence of gonadal hormone influences on dopaminergic function during puberty." Hormones and Behavior, Vol. 58(1), 122–137.

Kuzma, J. M. and Black, D. W. (2008). "Epidemiology, prevalence, and natural history of compulsive sexual behavior." The Psychiatric Clinics of North America, Vol.31(4), 603–611.

Lam, L. T., Peng, Z. W., Mai, J. C. and Jing, J. (2009). "Factors associated with Internet addiction among adolescents." Cyberpsychology & Behavior, Vol. 12(5):551–5.

Lansford, J. E., Yu, T., Erath, S. A., Pettit, G. S., Bates, J. E. and Dodge, K. A. (2010). "Developmental precursors of number of sexual partners from ages 16 to 22." Journal of Research on Adolescence, Vol. 20(3), 651–677.

Leung, L. (2004). "Net-generation attributes and seductive properties of the Internet as predictors of online activities and internet addiction." Cyberpsychology & Behavior, Vol. 7(3):333–48.

Lloyd, J., Doll, H., Hawton, K., Dutton, W. H., Geddes,

J.R., Goodwin, G. M. and Rogers, R. D. (2010). "How psychological symptoms relate to different motivations for gambling: An online study of internet gamblers." Biological Psychiatry, Vol. 68(8):733–40.

Markey, P. and Markey, C. (2011). "Pornography-seeking behaviors following midterm political elections in the United States: A replication of the challenge hypothesis." Computers in Human Behavior, Vol. 27(3), 1262–1264.

Mathy, R. M. and Cooper, A. (2003). "The duration and frequency of internet use in a nonclinical sample: Suicidality, behavioral problems, and treatment histories." Psychotherapy Theory Research Practice Training, Vol. 40(1), 125–135.

Mehroof, M. and Griffiths, M. D. (2010). "Online gaming addiction: The role of sensation seeking, self-control, neuroticism, aggression, state anxiety, and trait anxiety." Cyberpsychology, Behavior & Social Networks, Vol. 13(3):313–6.

Nelson, L. J., Padilla-Walker, L. M. and Carroll, J. S. (2010). "I believe it is wrong but I still do it: A comparison of religious young men who do versus do not use pornography." Psychology of Religion and Spirituality, Vol. 2(3), 136–147.

Ni X., Yan H., Chen S. and Liu Z. (2009). "Factors influencing internet addiction in a sample of freshmen university students in China." Cyberpsychology & Behavior, Vol. 12(3):327–30.

Oh, W. O. (2003). "Factors influencing internet addiction

tendency among middle school students in Gyeong-buk area." Taehan Kanho Hakhoe Chi, Vol. 33(8):1135–44.

Park, H. S, Kwon, Y. H. and Park, K. M. (2007). "Factors on internet game addiction among adolescents." Taehan Kanho Hakhoe Chi, Vol. 37(5):754–61.

Park, S. K., Kim, J. Y. and Cho, C. B. (2008). "Prevalence of Internet addiction and correlations with family factors among South Korean adolescents." Adolescence, Vol. 43(172):895–909.

Paul, B. (2009). "Predicting internet pornography use and arousal: The role of individual difference variables." Journal of Sex Research, Vol. 46(4), 344–357.

Perry, M., Accordino, M. P. and Hewes, R. L. (2007). "Investigation of internet use, sexual and nonsexual sensation seeking, and sexual compulsivity among college students." Sexual Addiction and Compulsivity, Vol. 14, 321–335.

Peter, J. and Valkenburg, P. M. (2011). "The use of sexually explicit Internet material and its antecedents: A longitudinal comparison of adolescents and adults." Archives of Sexual Behavior, Vol. 40 (5), 1015-1025.

Peter, J. and Valkenburg, P. M. (2010) "Processes underlying the effects of adolescents' use of sexually explicit internet material: The role of perceived realism." Communication Research, Vol. 37, 375–399.

Petersen, K. U., Weymann, N., Schelb, Y., Thiel, R. and Thomasius, R. (2009). "Pathological Internet use epidemiology, diagnostics, co-occurring disorders and treatment." Fortschr Neurological Psychiatry, Vol. 77(5):263–71.

Pinkerton, S. D., Bogart, L. M., Cecil, H. and Abramson, P. R. (2002). "Factors associated with masturbation in a collegiate sample." Journal of Psychology and Human Sexuality, Vol. 14(2–3), 103–121.

Popovic, M. (2011). "Pornography use and closeness with others in men." Archives of Sexual Behavior, Vol. 40(2), 449–456.

Reid, R. C., Stein, J. A. and Carpenter, B. N. (2011). "Understanding the roles of shame and neuroticism in a patient sample of hypersexual men." Journal of Nervous and Mental Disease, Vol. 199(4), 263–267.

Samenow, C. P. (2010). "A biopsychosocial model of hypersexual disorder/sexual addiction." Sexual Addiction and Compulsivity, Vol. 17(2), 69–81.

Sanchez-Carbonell, X., Beranuy, M., Castellana, M., Chamarro, A. and Oberst, U. (2008). "Internet and cellphone addiction: Passing fad or disorder?" Adicciones, Vol. 20(2):149–59.

Schmitz, J. M. (2005). "The interface between impulse control disorders and addictions: Are pleasure pathway responses shared neurobiological substrates?" Sexual Addiction and Compulsivity, Vol. 12(2), 149–168.

Seigfried-Spellar, K. C. and Rogers, M. K. (2010). "Low neuroticism and high hedonistic traits for female internet child pornography consumers." CyberPsychology, Behavior and Social Networking, Vol. 13(6), 629–635.

Seo, M., Kang, H. S. and Yom, Y. H. (2009). "Internet addiction and interpersonal problems in Korean adolescents." Computer, Informatics, Nursing, Vol. 27(4):226–33.

Seto, M. C. (2010). "Child pornography use and internet solicitation in the diagnosis of pedophilia." Archives of Sexual Behavior, Vol. 39(3), 591–593.

Skegg, K., Nada-Raja, S., Dickson, N. and Paul, C. (2010). "Perceived 'out of control' sexual behavior in a cohort of young adults from the Dunedin Multidisciplinary Health and Development Study." Archives of Sexual Behavior, Vol. 39(4), 968–978.

Song, X. Q., Zheng, L., Li, Y., Yu, D. X. and Wang, Z. Z. (2010). "Status of 'internet addiction disorder' (IAD) and its risk factors among first-grade junior students in Wuhan." Zhonghua Liu Xing Bing Xue Za Zhi, Vol. 31(1), 14-7

Strutherrs, W. M. (2009). Wired for Intimacy: How pornography hijacks the male brain. Downers Grove, Ill.: IVP Books.

Tau, G. Z. and Peterson, B. S. (2010). "Normal development of brain circuits." Neuropsychopharmacology, Vol. 35, 147–168.

Tsai, H. F., Cheng, S. H., Yeh, T. L., Shih, C. C., Chen, K.C., Yang, Y. C. and Yang, Y. K. (2009). "The risk factors of Internet addiction: A survey of university freshmen." Psychiatry Research, Vol. 167(3):294–9.

Tsitsika, A., Critselis, E., Janikian, M., Kormas, G. and Kafetzis, D. A. (2011). "Association between internet gambling and problematic internet use among adolescents." Journal of Gambling Studies, Vol. 27(3):389–400.

Tsitsika, A., Critselis, E., Kormas, G., Filippopoulou, A., Tounissidou, D., Freskou, A., Spiliopoulou, T., Louizou, A., Konstantoulaki E. and Kafetzis, D. (2009). "Internet use and misuse: A multivariate regression analysis of the predictive factors of
Internet use among Greek adolescents." European Journal of Pediatrics, Vol. 168(6):655–65.

Tsitsika, A., Critselis, E., Louizou, A., Janikian, M., Freskou, A., Marangou, E., Kormas, G. and Kafetzis, D. (2011). "Determinants of Internet addiction among adolescents: A case-control study." Scientific World Journal, Vol. 11:866–74.

Twohig, M. P., Crosby, J. M. and Cox, J. M. (2009). "Viewing Internet pornography: For whom is it problematic, how, and why?" Sexual Addiction and Compulsivity, Vol. 16(4), 25–266.

Van Rooij, A. J., Schoenmakers, T. M., Van de Eijnden, R. J. and Van de Mheen, D. (2010). "Compulsive Internet use: The role of online gaming and other internet applications." Journal of Adolescent Health, Vol. 47(1):51–7.

Velezmoro, R., Lacefield, K. and Roberti, J. W. (2010)."Perceived stress, sensation seeking, and college students' abuse of the Internet." Computers in Human Behavior, Vol. 26(6), 1526–1530.

Villella, C., Martinotti, G., Di Nicola, M., Cassano, M.,

La Torre, G., Gliubizzi, M. D., Messeri, I., Petruccelli, F., Bria, P., Janiri, L. and Conte, G. (2011). "Behavioural addictions in adolescents and young adults: Results from a prevalence study." Journal of Gambling Studies, Vol. 27(2):203–14.

Wang, H., Zhou, X., Lu, C., Wu, J., Deng, X. and Hong, L. (2011). "Problematic Internet use in high school students in Guangdong Province, China." PLoS One, Vol. 6(5)

Washton, A. and Boundy, D. (1989). Willpower's Not Enough: Recovering from addictions of every kind. New York: HarperPerrennial.

Ybarra, M. L., Finkelhor, D., Mitchell, K. J. and Wolak, J. (2009). "Associations between blocking, monitoring, and filtering software on the home computer and youth reported unwanted exposure to sexual material online." Child Abuse and Neglect, Vol. 33(12), 857–869.

Yellowlees, P. M. and Marks, S. (2007). "Problematic Internet use or Internet addiction?" Computers in Human Behavior, Vol. 23, 144–1453.

Yen, J. Y., Ko, C. H., Yen, C. F., Wu, H. Y. and Yang, M. J. (2007). "The comorbid psychiatric symptoms of Internet addiction: Attention deficit and hyperactivity disorder (ADHD), depression, social phobia, and hostility." Journal of Adolescence Health, Vol. 41(1):93–8.

Yen, J., Yen, C., Chen, C., Tang, T. and Ko, C. (2009). "The association between adult ADHD symptoms and Internet addiction among college students: The gender difference." CyberPsychology and Behavior, Vol. 12(2),187–191.

Yoo, H. J., Cho, S. C., Ha, J., Yune, S. K., Kim, S. J., Hwang, J., Chung, A., Sung, Y. H. and Lyoo, I. K. (2004). "Attention deficit hyperactivity symptoms and Internet addiction." Psychiatry Clinical Neuroscience, Vol. 58(5):487–94.

Zhang, Z. H., Hao, J. H., Yang, L. S., Zhang, X. J., Sun, Y.H., Hu, C. L., Ye, D. Q. and Tao, F. B. (2009). "The relationship between emotional, physical abuse and Internet addiction disorder among middle school students." Zhonghua Liu Xing Bing Xue Za Zhi, Vol. 30(2):115–8

Special thanks to the Boyer Foundation,
Ilan Almog, and all of our donors for
making this book possible.

FIGHT THE NEW DRUG